RELATIONSHIPS
Done Easy

Creating Delicious Possibilities

Kathy Williams & Friends

Happy Publishing

RELATIONSHIPS DONE EASY

www.RelationshipsDoneEasy.com

Copyright 2017 by Kathy Williams

ISBN 978-0-9983708-2-8

Editor Kathy Williams

Cover Design by Nada Orlic

Interior Design by Roseanna White
www.RoseannaWhiteDesigns.com

First Edition

Published by Happy Publishing, www.HappyPublishing.net

Contents

Preface

Have your relationships been fun at first, and then full of frustration? Have you had trouble finding that "special someone," or kissed more than a few princes (or princesses), only to have them turn into frogs later? What would it take to bring out the best in each other, instead of the worst? Imagine having a relationship that expands the ease, joy, and possibilities that you and your partner experience each day. What if your relationship could continually climb to new heights instead of beginning on a high note and descending from there?

We created this book to invite you to that possibility. Relationships really can expand your life beyond anything you have ever experienced before. Unfortunately, that's not what we see most of the time. More often, people experience drudgery, frustration, communication challenges, and unmet expectations. Is this you? Perhaps by asking a few questions and applying some simple, practical tools, you too can create a joyful, nurturing, expansive relationship. With some shifts in perspective, it might be easier than you think.

Have you ever seen people interact and wondered, *Why do they stay together? They seem to carry more resentment than appreciation for each other*! On the other hand, have you seen couples who live together in bliss and enjoyment, long after the honeymoon? What differentiates the

relationships that thrive from the ones that disintegrate into frustration, resentment, and passive aggression?

When you reflect on your life, can you find many examples of couples who truly enjoyed each other? Or just a few? None at all?

What could you create if you had even better role models?

Whether you're single, recently coupled, or have been married for decades, the authors in these pages have tools, insights, and anecdotes to bring ease and intimacy that maybe you've only dreamed of. They don't hold back. Writing in their own voices, with grace and vulnerability, they express their challenges, successes, and what they used that helped them along the way. Some have been married for decades, some recently tied the knot, and others divorced when they realized they were living a life that wasn't for them. You'll find chapters that offer questions and exercises to attract an amazing partner or ideas to make divorce smoother and others that detail the journey from relationship frustration to ease and communion. One chapter delightfully expresses relationship ups and downs from both the husband's and the wife's perspectives.

Just as you are unique, your relationships are too. The diversity of authors from across the globe—male/female/gay/straight/married/unmarried—offers a smorgasbord, so that no matter where you are in your life, on any given day you can return to the book and find an insight, a gem, or something to apply.

You could read this book once and apply the questions and suggestions to enhance your current relationship or attract a new one. Or, if you'd like to get the most out of it, pick it up from time to time, reread a chapter, and find something new. Different parts of the book may be more useful at different points in your relationship journey; the next time around, you might discover a tip or suggestion that was previously irrelevant, but is now useful and will create the change you are looking for! To make the most of your reading experience, write in the margins, highlight, or jot down your awarenesses. Please make this book your own. Try things out. Experiment and see what works for you!

We would love to hear from you! Let us know what worked, what questions you have, and what you'd like to see more of. Email: RelationshipsDoneEasy@gmail.com

What invitation can we be to create a new reality with relationships on the planet?

I wonder...

With great gratitude and a sprinkling of joy,

Kathy Williams

A few notes:

The authors in this book all have a background in Access Consciousness®, a worldwide movement that offers practical tools to empower people. Their stories reflect their own experiences and do not necessarily reflect the points of view of Access Consciousness. Find out more at www.accessconsciousness.com

You won't see "love" very often, which is unusual for a book on relationships. That's because we each have our own ideas about what love means. Some of the authors will elaborate more. Often you'll see the word "desire" instead of "want," (a word with 27 definitions which indicate lack). There may be some other words you see, or don't see, that you have questions about. Please contact us if that piques your curiosity!

Question Day

BY SARAH GRANDINETTI

I sat there stunned, wishing I could pick up each word that fell out of my mouth and put them back in one by one. I closed my eyes and started asking myself what the heck I was thinking to utter those words to the man I loved. I've never wanted to disempower him from being the provider...the role he had played in our marriage for 18 years! Who was I to act like I could come in and take over that role? *Please, sweet husband, I'm too tired to fight.*

Rewind.

I had just finished a long work day in the salon. I'm a hair stylist. I own and run my salon with several very talented women. On this particular day, I had seen 11 clients. I was exhausted. I was so ready to get home and see my family and collapse in my bed. But then it hit me! Oh snaps! I hadn't made a plan for that evening's dinner! My husband, Steve, was all set to pick up the kids and get them home, but I had completely boneheaded on a plan to feed our four kids... and subsequently us! Gosh, what was falling through the cracks was seeming kind of major and I didn't know how much steam I had left in my tank to "do it all." I walked out of the salon that night with a shit ton of judgment of myself! *What kind of mother doesn't have a plan on what to feed her family? Now that I think about it, when was the last time I checked their homework? When was that "Life of a Zebra" diorama due again? Aren't we supposed to be shopping for a prom dress right now? What else am I missing? Something's gotta give...and it can't be me and my body!*

See, I had gone back to work full time, which I hadn't done in years, to increase my family's bottom line. I had previously worked three days a week and saw my income from behind the chair as just an added bonus—my husband had always provided everything else. We had suffered some financial setbacks, and it was time that I started to take more of an active role in our finances...totally welcomed by him because the poor man was stressed out! He was trying to hold it all together and not worry me in any way—until he met his breaking point. It was my turn. I had to finally look at myself in the mirror and start to peel back the layers of lies that I had bought about myself and what I was capable of, and go after what I was intended for. The interesting part? He always knew that about me. He always saw me as a shining star who could change the world, but for some unknown reason, I believe we were both too nervous to really look at it.

As I loaded my purse and the uneaten lunch from hours ago into my car, I felt that damn frog in my throat. I wanted to cry. I was aware that I was so excited about how busy I had become in just a short time of making the demand for things to change financially and I knew that it was what I had asked for, so the tears weren't coming from a sad place. Looking back, I believe my body and I knew that day that I couldn't continue working like this and worrying about my family at night. I knew I was struggling with society's definitions of a "good mom," and that part of me was still buying that framework built by the 1950's housewife. She did dishes in a dress and pantyhose with her hair coiffed and had dinner on the table when her hard-working husband walked through the door every night. I didn't know how I was possibly going to keep up my image of the mom who kept it all together while going after the things I knew were possible.

One thing that always helps me is to ask questions, and not to look for answers! The tools I've picked up from Access Consciousness® have allowed me to create space to look for possibilities and stop me from going down the path of conclusion and wrongness for what I was choosing...in this case, being a "bad mom/wife."

On my drive home, I started asking a ton of questions. I was asking what it would take to have my home life supported brilliantly and with ease and still have space for me to chase my dreams. I had the awareness that I also wanted my dear husband/best friend to be able to follow his dreams and not get caught on the sidelines of "my life." My awareness quickly turned to him and what he wants out of life—where he might be giving up on what he knew was possible as well. He had built quite a career in the restaurant industry, but I knew that he had always dreamed of more. I started allowing his dreams to flow through me. (Insert more tears...the happy kind.) He has always worked so hard for our family, and I didn't ever want to make him feel irrelevant or like he had to cut off any part of him to support me! How were we going to tackle this? What else was possible that I hadn't even considered?

As I walked through the front door, I noticed something immediately. It was a smell. One that I recognized, but couldn't place. I was famished, so was I turning the smell of my son's dirty gym socks into a savory treat just to feed my senses? I walked further into the house and passed by the dining room table, where my daughter Talia was steadily finishing up her homework. My son, Steven II, was on the computer typing up a paper. My oldest daughter, Kylee, was in her room studying and my youngest, Shyla, was in the kitchen helping Daddy clean up from dinner. My eyes met my husband's, and he could instantly tell something was up with me. And, like he often does, he came to me and offered a sweet, melt into my arms, supportive hug! I rested my head on his broad shoulders and just exhaled... like I had done for 18 years. I would've stayed there longer had I not been reminded of that mouthwatering smell coming from somewhere in the kitchen! I pulled back from the hug and started to look for the source of the smell. He smirked and asked if I was hungry. I nodded and pulled up a stool to the kitchen island.

This man proceeded to pull a homemade chicken pot pie from the oven! My mouth dropped open (from drooling and shock), and I sat there in gratitude! He pulled a plate from the cupboard and started to dish me out a serving of that yummy goodness. My eyes were gleaming with anticipation, and I could tell he was so excited for me to try it as well. And that was when I said it: the question that I thought would change us forever...And, well, in a way, I guess it did.

I took one bite of the deliciousness on my plate, and without actually putting together a logical thought, I turned to my family's breadwinner/dragon slayer and said, "Wow, Babe, this is delicious! I wonder what it would take for me to replace your income so that you could be home with kids and make dinners like this EVERY night?!"

Silence.

Eyes closed (other areas clenched!), I sat in silence and anticipated his response. This sweet man pondered for a moment and said, "I could do that!"

If I could have recorded my internal dialogue right then, I could have sold it to play as the background track of the latest thriller! The screams that were happening in my head blew my whole world wide open!! This man was willing to leave his career to create ease in our lives?? Say, Whaatttttt??? The idea seemed preposterous! But, boy did it feel super light!! Another tool that we often use in Access Consciousness is called "light and heavy." It's easily explained that whatever is true for you will make you feel lighter and whatever is a lie for you will make you feel heavier. This, my friends, was super light!

Here's the coolest part: that one question opened up doors to discussions that we hadn't been willing to have before the question was asked. Imagine this: two people living

Sarah Grandinetti

side by side, supporting each other, loving each other, being present for each other...but both buying a lie—the lie that the other one believed strongly in the "roles" of this society. So, they went about their days working their asses off and simultaneously judging themselves for doing so, all to uphold what was a lie for them.

Steve and I had decided somewhere, maybe from the roles of our parents, that the husband's job was to make the money and the wife's was to take care of the home. When we bought that as true and real, we cut ourselves off from what was possible for us, our family and our financial future. I was so worried that if I "out-created" him that his ego would be bruised, so I consistently made just enough to be under the amount that he made. He, on the other hand, never wanted to dream big about what he could create with his life because he didn't want to invite the possibility of losing my respect if he were to suggest that I carry the finances for a while so he could chase a dream. Yet, both of us were essentially living a lie. I knew deep down that I could create beyond what I was already creating, and he knew that he had more to give the world than his current job evoked. Not to mention, he loves child rearing, and he's really good at it! Who comes home from a long day at work, picks up four kids, gets them started on homework annnnnndddd "throws together" a pot pie? There are probably many people with this skill set, most that I have yet to meet, and all that aren't me! I love my kids, and I love cooking (on the weekends), but there is something about the weeknight pressure that was spinning me out at the time when I was also trying to work more. Yet, I absolutely loved being at work and bringing home bigger and bigger paychecks! That lit me UP!

There was a time shortly after this question fell out of my mouth that my husband asked me to go grocery shopping. This was not foreign to me. I had done it many times before. The interesting thing that occurred this time was that it was like he was speaking Chinese to me. I hate grocery shopping, and as he started to run down the list of what we needed in the kitchen that morning, I started to well up with tears! (No, seriously!) I couldn't physically force myself back into the box that that question had exploded me out of. He looked up from taking inventory of the pantry and saw my tears. Immediately he came and took the list out of my hand, said not to worry about it and that he would handle it after he got off work. It was honestly one of the sweetest moments of my 18-year relationship with this man. He saw me trying to stuff myself back in... and he wasn't having it! He told me to spend the day taking care of some of the things that had to be done for the new businesses that I was launching and knew that's where my time was best spent. What a gift!

Since the day that we now refer to as "Question Day," we have had the deepest conversations of our marriage. Just when you think you know someone better than you know yourself, they tell you that they would love to be able to dabble in real estate, or own their own deli, or fix up cars! I've begun writing two business plans and have watched as a dream came to fruition...I am now holding workshops in my salon to inspire women. That one question opened up so many possibilities, and the funny part is that if you look back at the question, I haven't actually replaced his income yet. He hasn't quit his job. We were just able to perceive the energy of it and started to create from there!

Relationships aren't always the cup of tea that you dream about on your wedding day. We have definitely been served our dose of difficulty and struggle. The thing that supports us the most is that we're not only best friends who don't ever give up on each other, but we are always seeking to know more about the other person. We choose to co-create our future, and it isn't ever a competition, but more like an invitation. Through this experience, we've learned just how important it is to ask questions—always. It seems so dang simple, but it's just not how we are entrained. In school, you are marked wrong if you don't come up with the right answer, teaching us and ingraining in us that seeking the answer is what is valuable. What if everything you ever wanted to create was just a few questions away? What if all you ever needed to have the life or the relationship you truly desire is the energy of what that is? What if a question could take you there, and you could start "having it" before it even showed up? What if these questions could give you a sense of space that you haven't allowed yourself to be aware was even possible? What if it's all available to you if you just ask? What if one question, asked with a mouthful of chicken pot pie, could blast your world WIDE OPEN?

What if? I'm just sayin'…

About the Author
Sarah Grandinetti

Sarah Grandinetti is the mother of of four children, a brilliant writer, and a dynamic facilitator. The owner of two successful businesses: Salon Mix and Being You Beauty, Sarah's desire to inspire and empower people to choose more, to actualize their dreams and know the beauty they are has a depth and breadth that touches people on many levels. While her work as a stylist involves physical beauty, Sarah's target is to pull the inner beauty out of her clients and to help them believe in themselves and see possibilities. The realization that most women don't even remember the last time they felt beautiful lead Sarah to create workshops to help women tap into their beauty—inside and out. If you would like to have your life catapulted toward everything you have been desiring, Sarah Grandinetti offers a possibility unlike anyone else.

This is what people are saying:

"What can I tell you about Sarah Grandinetti? She is so many things; a writer, a business owner, a dynamic creator, a mother, a wife, a healer. She is all of these things, but what is most relevant to me is the way she listens. The kind of listening when you know she is hearing all of the layers, not just what you put on the surface. She hears the place where your voice quivers because you are pretending everything is ok, where anger flashes, where you hold your breath. She listens. And in that listening, she creates a space of no judgment and total caring for you in a way that is not often given in this world. In her presence, the things you have decided are unchangeable suddenly have space and possibility. And yet she will not push you to change it, with grace and allowance Sarah is just present for you. She listens." - CS

Are you asking for change? Sarah would love to hear from you! Email her at Sarah@beingyoubeauty.com

Or visit www.beingyoubeauty.com

Men Aren't Just Hairy Women and Other Surprising Realizations

BY KATHY WILLIAMS

As the legendary Dale Carnegie said so well, the choice to be "hearty in your approbation and lavish in your praise" is a key attribute of thriving relationships. In 2015, I interviewed a handful of men about what they consider to be "honoring" to prepare for a radio show on *Imperfect Brilliance* entitled "Honoring the Men in our Lives." To my surprise, the first thing they each mentioned was "appreciation." They really want to hear that we are grateful for them and what they do. (Mention of a warm meal on the table was close behind!)

If it is that simple, how come it can seem so hard? Relationship expert Alison Armstrong says that women hold men to high standards; we expect them to behave as the perfect woman would! It's almost as though we consider them hairy women, instead of realizing they have different strengths—and not just their biceps. We are wired differently. As a man once quipped to me, "Men only think of one thing at a time, and most of the time there's only one thing on our minds." Women are strong in what Armstrong calls "diffuse awareness," the capacity that allows us to multitask and keep track of many things at once. Most men are better at single focus—the attention required in finding and shooting a deer...quite different from making a lunch while quizzing a kid about spelling words and making a mental note about which report to print and take to work. This means I can't expect to have a great conversation with my husband, Dave, while he is packing for an upcoming trip or driving to dinner at a new restaurant. He is single focused. If I wait until he's finished packing or until we have arrived at the restaurant, our conversation will flow much better. While I haven't found everything Alison Armstrong says to be true, this one point created a world of ease in my relationship.

Point! That's another difference in communication styles— men usually look for a point (and something to solve) while women are happy to talk just for the sake of connection. So the unsolicited advice they give isn't because they think we're dumb or incapable of handling our life or business. I used to get annoyed with such advice, thinking, *I'm not stupid; I know what to do. Does he think I'm an idiot?* He was giving me advice because men love to find solutions and provide for the women in their lives. The desire to provide can also include actions: it can actually be a gift to both the woman and the man to allow him to carry a heavy box or to put a carry-on bag in the overhead compartment if he offers. Imagine the feeling of having someone receive and appreciate your kind gesture, instead of turning you away by saying, "No thanks, I can do it."

Once I became aware of the ways women make men feel wrong by expecting them to behave like well-mannered hairy females, I started to observe these dynamics at the grocery store, in airports, and with people I know. Emasculating tendencies abound and include eye rolling, ridiculing his passion for a sports team or enjoyment of shoot-em-up movies, even criticizing the ways he dresses or does daily tasks. I once observed this scenario between a couple at a gate just before my flight boarded: the man went off to check on something, then came back and reported on what he'd found. Clearly dissatisfied with the way he had done it, the woman rolled her eyes, shoved the baby at him, and went to do it herself, leaving him a little baffled and shellshocked. Similarly, last Christmas at a party, a husband beamed about how he had looked some things up on the iPhone for his wife. "Yes, but you forgot this part," she responded, and her superior attitude deflated him in front of my eyes.

Man or woman, in our culture we often buy into the unrealistic idea that if we find the one right person for us we'll be happy—even "complete." Eventually we find out that the "right person" has flaws; they leave their socks on the floor, talk too much, or come home late. In response, some of us leave our back door metaphorically open— committed, but only partially—keeping an eye out just in case an even better "right" person comes along. Over time the tension builds and maybe we leave this person or try to change them. Yet the next person has flaws too. After all, who doesn't?

Perhaps resigned to the relationship we are in, we wait to see if our partner will do something awful or stupid enough to compel us to move on (or even leave us so we don't have to leave them). Still other couples, committed "til death do us part" pine for something different, but stay—slowly dying inside because it would take time, energy, or money to change (or leave), and they've already invested so much. What if, after thorough reflection, if a relationship was not working, both parties could discuss it without drama or having to make the other person wrong? "Ok, that was fun. Now it's limiting us . . . . What would we like to choose now?" And are there ways to nurture the loving feelings shared early in relationships, so they continue and grow as time goes on?

What if relationships didn't even require "hard work" to be fun? Listening to a podcast one day, I heard the comment, "We don't work on our relationship. We just keep going forward until something doesn't work. At that point, we look at it together and ask, 'What else can I be or do here that would work for both of us?'" It doesn't require one of the partners to be "wrong" or the other "right"; both are a team. This echoes the way my husband and I work together. The more we flow with what is working, the more things flow harmoniously. The more we resist and turn our attention to what's not right, the more that shows up, confirming Jung's line, "What you resist persists."

Like many people, I used to carry around my "hurts" in a backpack of emotional upsets, filing away each criticism my husband made for future reference. Every once in awhile,

I'd dig around and revive painful memories: a criticism about my body from 2005, or one about my driving from 2010.... You can imagine the effect this had on my mood, and how it colored our interactions! I had evidence of the fact that my husband didn't love or value me (even if that "evidence" was scattered comments from our 13 years together). The more I focused on painful words and situations from the past, the more they tainted our present. It was almost like bird poop on my glasses. If my glasses are covered in crappy memories, they certainly limit my ability to see life (and him) as it is NOW. Dave is not the person he was in 2005 or 2010, and I'm not who I was then either! Because we constantly have new awarenesses and experiences, we are not even the same people we were last week! When my mind is clouded by old hurts, I wallow in the cesspool of painful thinking and no longer see that we are not the people we were years (or weeks) ago.

What do I do if those old grievances pop up? Reminding myself that those words were simply a snapshot of how he was thinking at a moment in time reduces their significance. I also love to ask, "What am I making significant that isn't?" This question has a way of reducing (or eliminating) any upsets I may have been holding. We all have moments when we say thoughtless things, and our words in those moments generally reveal more about our frustrated or irritated inner state than our true feelings about the other person. To focus on them is sort of like fixating on a few misplaced brush strokes in a portrait instead of on the beauty of the whole picture.

One of the tools I learned from Access Consciousness® is to "uncreate" my relationship (and everything it has

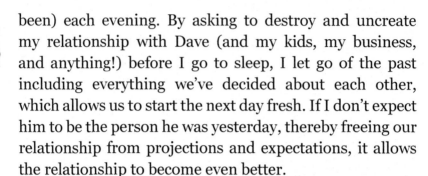

been) each evening. By asking to destroy and uncreate my relationship with Dave (and my kids, my business, and anything!) before I go to sleep, I let go of the past including everything we've decided about each other, which allows us to start the next day fresh. If I don't expect him to be the person he was yesterday, thereby freeing our relationship from projections and expectations, it allows the relationship to become even better.

In Access, we have a saying: "Your point of view creates your reality." Psychologist Mavis Karn articulated the subtle obvious when she said, "Whatever we are choosing to believe, we can find evidence for." I may have been able to find plenty of evidence that my husband didn't love me when I used past criticisms as proof, but when I believe he does value me, I always find plenty of memories to support that. Focusing on the hurts always feels worse than focusing on what IS working about our relationship.

Appreciating what works and bringing attention to what we enjoy about each other has been fundamental in nurturing my marriage. When Dave was in medical residency with long hours and a heavy workload, it was a stressful time for both of us. So, I started a gratitude notebook, listing five to ten things I appreciated about him each day. I like to say that everything works better with gratitude. This is especially true about relationships! One definition of appreciation is "to go up in value." When I focus on the things about Dave that add to the richness of my life, it increases my loving feelings toward him.

In our 20's, when we had been dating for about a year, one of us had the idea—I think we read it somewhere—to list out everything we'd like the other person to change.

Once we had taken inventory, we went to a nearby park to share our findings. Expressing what we found wrong with each other brought up so much pain and upset that I'm surprised we stayed together! If we had listed all the qualities and characteristics that we were grateful for, it would have had quite a different effect.

Now I have a reminder on my phone that signals me daily: "Appreciate Dave." When it does, I might send him a little text, silently recognize him in my mind, or send some gratitude from afar. As a partner, I can appreciate all of him, not just the parts that are how I would like him to be. What do I mean? I don't share Dave's love for fishing, but I can appreciate how being out on the water and doing what he enjoys adds to his life. I don't love finding his dirty shirt on the bedroom floor; but as I put it in the laundry, I can have gratitude that he's in my life and he's around—not traveling far away, or leaving that shirt on someone else's floor.

Likewise, the fact that I'm in the relationship doesn't mean I have to abandon the things I love. In the beginning, Dave couldn't understand why I love to take classes and expand my skill sets. His attitude was, *more expenses and more time away from me!* After a while, he said, "I get it! That's your fishing." If we felt the need to let go of everything that wasn't a mutual interest, we would have very limited lives!

For many of my clients, as careers take off and families grow, attention to their partners diminishes. If this is happening in your life, perhaps it could be useful to explore how much time you would like to spend together. For some couples, 20 minutes daily is enough, while others require a more concentrated date night or outing together every

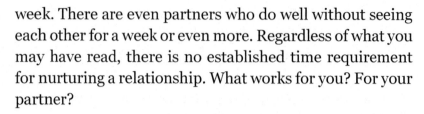

week. There are even partners who do well without seeing each other for a week or even more. Regardless of what you may have read, there is no established time requirement for nurturing a relationship. What works for you? For your partner?

Dave and I like to have a weekly date night, and it's fun for us to throw in something extra, like a whale watch or a hike in a new location. What I love even more is to get away, just the two of us, leaving the kids with my parents, a sitter, or someone I've worked out a trade with. A weekend away from home can work wonders for us when life has started to feel routine. What would be fun for you to do together? Create a list of activities: batting cages, the swap meet, a symphony, a night outside with a star map.... The sky is not even the limit. The only limitations are the ones you've put in place! What keeps you from the fun you'd like to have together? Money? Time? Frustration with each other? Kids? What are some creative solutions you could use to work around those roadblocks?

On the other end of the spectrum, I have clients who are retired and lament, "We do everything together; I can't get away from him." As they complain about not having time alone, I ask if they've ever expressed their desire for alone time with their partner. If your "enjoyable other" doesn't know you require some space, it may be easier to broach the subject when you are not bursting at the seams with discontent, but rather, in a space of appreciation. I often suggest starting small, perhaps by choosing a yoga class, going to workout, or shopping—which often sends men running in another direction. Even if both of you go to the gym, you can be in completely different areas, one doing weights, while the other does cardio or takes a class. Designating a night for friends or having a weekly coffee date with a friend can also work wonders for refreshing the staleness of too much time spent together.

If you're a couple who does spend a lot of time together, could you point yourselves in a unified direction? A couple I facilitate frequently has been happily married for almost 60 years. They are both highly involved in their church and its outreach programs, but instead of doing all the same activities, they take different roles, so they are not bumping elbows or constantly interacting with each other as they work toward the same target. This gives them something to talk about and bounce ideas around, but having different positions keeps it interesting.

The quality of interaction with my husband has made a bigger difference than the amount of time we spend together. Because I have a business that I love, it can be easy for me to get sucked into computer work or phone calls at any time of the day. I've noticed that when I'm willing to turn my attention away from my devices and look at Dave, it gives the message that I value him and what he has to say. Keeping my attention fixed on my screen and only muttering short responses to his questions sends a very different message. We've all seen those people at a restaurant who, instead of engaging in conversation, stare at their phones throughout the meal. I love my phone as much as the next person, but to keep the temptation to "stay connected" at bay, I've begun leaving it in the car when we go to a restaurant or keeping it plugged in while we eat dinner at home. Any work or calls can wait an hour, while I'm present with something that is a huge contribution to my life—him!

Over the last 13 years, we have taken many actions to improve our relationship. We've read books, gone to counseling, embarked on a "relationship course," and taken a tantra workshop along with a number of other things. What I've shared in these pages seems to have made the greatest positive impact. Our relationship has seen it's share of stressful times, but with respect, gratitude, time for just the two of us, and undivided attention, we've been able to successfully navigate the bumps in the road, and move on to smoother sailing. By acknowledging that we are each unique and won't always agree, we've created the space to be more curious about each other than critical. Curiosity and gratitude have replaced our early patterns of trying to control the other—which never worked, and only created massive frustration! From the space of non-judgment, our perspectives come together and create something even greater than either of us had imagined. In that sense, 1 + 1 = Infinite Possibilities. With an attitude of curiosity, a sprinkling of gratitude and by asking questions, *anything* can change. If anything can change, what would *you* like to create?

About the Author
Kathy Williams

Armed with a variety of tools for transformation, Kathy Williams takes great joy in watching clients' lives evolve from stress and indecision to clarity and flow. While dancing as a professional ballerina, she began working in the field of mind-body transformation and became a yoga instructor in 2000. Over the past decade, she has worked as a certified Transformative Coach (through Michael Neill's Supercoach Academy), and Viniyoga Therapist, and she loves connecting with clients all over the world using these skills and the tools of Access Consciousness®. Initially, she used the tools of Neuro-Linguistic Programing and EFT (Emotional Freedom Technique), Reiki and Pranic Healing. When Kathy discovered Access Consciousness, the tools streamlined her sessions (and her life) with quicker, more effective results.

As an Access Consciousness Certified Facilitator, Kathy facilitates Access Bars®, Body Processes, Energetic Facelift Classes, "The Foundation" and specialty classes. Her retreats on the island of Maui (and other fun places) include Access Consciousness, Yoga, or the 3 Principles as articulated by Syd Banks. Kathy believes that each person has a well of wisdom and capacities that nobody else on the planet has in quite the same way and that when you tap into your uniqueness and your abilities, you expand the beauty and the inspiration on the planet. To her, one of the greatest gifts is hearing and seeing clients change their financial flows, bodies, relationships, and lives.

Kathy is published in the best-selling books, *I'm Having It,* and *Possibilities in Parenting* and she is presently writing books on tantra and emotional freedom. Hear her on *Imperfect Brilliance* radio show on iTunes Podcast or Youtube, or live on Mondays on the Inspired Choices Network online. Using the tools that she shares with clients, Kathy created a thriving business and life in Hawaii. On weekends, you'll find her hiking the tropical forests of Maui with three handsome men, two little and one big.

Kathy would love to hear from you! What's up in your relationship? What are your targets and your challenges? Email her for a complimentary 30 minute session to focus on your relationship—better yet, text her at 808-268-8708. For a speaking event or personal retreat, or to create a workshop in your area, email RelationshipsDoneEasy@gmail.com. To see a list of existing workshops or retreats, please visit www.clarityspace.org or www.iotransformation.com.

Her Access Consciousness events can be found at www.KathyWilliams.accessconsciousness.com.

Want to connect on Facebook? Find Kathy Williams, Author, Speaker, Transformation Agent

The List

BY BRET RUSHIA

Have you ever looked at what it is that you would truly like to create with your life?

You are an infinite being with infinite choice and infinite possibility. You have the ability to perceive, know, be, and receive anything and everything. It is simply who you be. Everything that is not currently working in your life is a place where you are pretending not to be, know, perceive, or receive something.

What can you ask for in a relationship that would contribute to your life becoming greater?

Stumped? Well then, now's the time to go shopping for your reality! Look at the lives of people you know. Look around at other people's relationships. Look around for qualities you've always dreamed of...and ask for them. What do other people have that you would like for yourself? Do you know someone who has a partner who is in total allowance of them? If so, ask for someone who is in total allowance of you! Just make sure you ask for only the parts and pieces that would work for you and not for the whole relationship because if you ask for it, it will show up. What could you add to your list that would make your life and relationships a constant source of joy?

Do you desire energies in a relationship that don't even seem to exist here on the planet? Don't forget to ask for those too! If you're reading this, I'm gonna guess that you're someone who would like to create something greater than what is currently here. What do you know is possible that nobody else knows is possible that if you asked for it would create a greater reality for all of us?

Ask and you shall receive is one of the truths of the universe. As an infinite being when you ask a question it sets the entire universe into motion to fulfill your request. What is currently showing up in your life is everything you've been asking for. Is it what you would truly like to create?

How does this work? Well, when you say, "I'm sick and tired of this relationship," what does that create? Phoom! There goes your energy! You have now officially begun to create you as "sick and tired." Welcome to sleeping 12 hours a day, having no energy, and getting your body sick. Is that really what you would like to create?

I had a friend who was asking the universe for "a fun guy to play with in bed." A week later she got a yeast infection. When she had asked for "a fun guy to play with in bed" the universe gave her exactly that, but with a slightly different spelling…"a fungi to play with in bed." Once she had that awareness, she could ask for something else that worked better for her. Her yeast infection quickly cleared up, and she found some fun playmates to play with in bed who would nurture her.

Your choices create. Your desires and the questions you ask actualize in the world, it just never shows up the way you think it will. Also, the universe is extremely literal, so be aware of what you're asking, or you might end up with a yeast infection, or even worse, a loving, nurturing relationship where you empower each other to be all of you without limitation! YUCK!

You, my friend, are the creator of everything in your life.

Let me say that again in a bigger font (for emphasis):

You are the creator of everything in your life.

Have you ever acknowledged that? Luckily, it includes the good things in your life and even more luckily, the bad and ugly things in your life. Why is that even more lucky? Well, that means if you've created even the bad and ugly things in your life then you are the one with the power. The bad and ugly didn't just happen to you. You created it. If you've created that, then what else could you create?

Every bad and ugly relationship you've ever had has been your creation! Isn't that a relief? For everything in your life that you acknowledge that you're the creator of, you gain the choice to change it or choose something different.

Now I'm not saying that when people do mean and nasty things that you're the creator of that. They are the ones choosing to do mean and nasty. What I am saying is that if you're with someone who does mean and nasty things, you have the choice whether or not to have that person in your life anymore.

When you feel stuck with something, acknowledge and celebrate your creations: "Wow. I'm awesome! I can sure create some crappy relationships! I am a grand and glorious creator! If I can create that, what else can I create?"

And from there, whatever you do, don't ask a silly question like:

"What would it take to create a truly great relationship?"

If you have something come up in your life over and over and over again, there is some part of the creation of it that you have not acknowledged. There is some awareness that you have that you are not acknowledging.

Awareness is the source of joy. If you're miserable anywhere in your life (or in your relationship), there's awareness that you can tap into that will lighten up your world! You, my friend, are aware. You know things that others just don't know. It's who you be. It's part of that whole "infinite being" thing I was blabbing on about earlier. That is the truth of you.

When you're functioning from infinite being, you're happy and everything works in your life (though not in the way you think it will).

When you're not functioning as an infinite being, you are functioning from a lie which inevitably makes you miserable.

Every time you acknowledge the truth of you as an infinite being, your world gets more happy and joyful.

In even simpler terms:

A lie = heavy, miserable, bored, depressed

What's true = light, airy, expansive, enthusiastic, joyful

Feeling heavy about relationships? Ask, "What's the lie here, spoken or unspoken?"

How do you know when you've got what the lie is? You'll become more happy, expanded, joyful and you'll probably even laugh. If you laugh, you've definitely got it!

When you're laughing, you're more of you, the infinite being.

"How much laughter can we have in this relationship?"

So this brings us back to the question...

What would you like to create with your life?

Would you like to have a relationship? Would you like to just have casual sex? What would you like? If nothing was wrong and nothing was right, what would work for you? What would you truly like to create?

When asking for someone to show up in your life, one thing you might want to do is create a list. This isn't just any list. This is a shopping list for what you truly desire.

There are two sections to the list: "What I would like this person to be" and "What I would not like this person to be."

The "What I would like this person to be" section is where you get to put down everything you've always desired a person to be in relationship. The sky isn't even the limit. What would you like this person to be? Would you like them to be kind to themselves and others? Would you like them to be kind to you? Would you like them to be great in bed? Contribute lots and lots of money to your life? To honor you with every choice? To acknowledge the gift that you be in their life?

For the second section of the list, you're going to write down everything you wouldn't like this person to be, or "What I would not like this person to be." This part is just as important (if not even more important) than the list of everything you would like. When Gary Douglas, founder of Access Consciousness®, created the list that brought in his first wife, he only wrote down the things that he would like the person to be. Yes, he got everything he desired her to be, but he also got a whole lot of stuff that was horrendous for him. For wife number two, he added a section of everything he wouldn't like the person to be. This time, she was everything he desired, and she did not have the traits he put in his "wouldn't like" category. He did make one mistake, though; in his list, he put "somebody who will fight life's battles with me." The universe is very literal, and it gave him someone who fought with him constantly. He meant fight life's battles side by side, but the universe heard "fight with me," and that's exactly what he got.

This section of the list is quite easy. You can find inspiration for what you don't want in relationship almost everywhere. You can start with your life and past relationships. Look through all of those crappy relationships and write down all of the traits you didn't like about all of those people. Look to your parents. What traits do they have that you definitely wouldn't like in a relationship?

★ someone who will nag me

★ someone who will just watch TV all day

★ someone who doesn't create

★ someone stupid

★ someone who will ignore me

★ someone who is selfish

Notice how it's much easier to find all the things you wouldn't like? Weird, huh?

So once you've written a whole bunch of stuff down, look over your list at each item and ask, "Is this something that I truly desire?"

In this world, we're taught to desire and live from what other people desire of us, what they require of us, and what they need from us. We are rarely, if ever, asked what we would like to have and create as our lives. With this list, that is what you are asking, item by item: "What do I truly desire to have as my life?" and "What would I truly like to have as a relationship?" Simply cross off everything on your list that you find isn't what you truly desire.

The next question you want to ask for each item is, "Is there any limitation that this would create?" I can't tell you how much pain, suffering, and weirdness you'll avoid if you do this step. The last thing you want to end up with is someone who will fight you all the time instead of side by side with you, just because of what you wrote down. Your words create. Asking, "What will this create?" and being aware of the energy of that choice is a great way to make sure you're getting what you truly desire.

Be specific, but also open-ended. For instance, if you put "someone who has a Mercedes" on your list, it limits what the universe can deliver to you, narrowing it down to this one specific thing that truly doesn't matter in creating your life. Instead, you could put something more open-ended like, "has a sense of wealth and a generosity of spirit." Now, this could include the person owning a Mercedes, but it also includes the possibilities of SO MUCH MORE. In the first example, the person could have a Mercedes and be a total miserly asshole who never even lets you in it. In the next scenario, the person may not have a Mercedes, but they may have a Bentley and with their generosity of spirit, they just might give it to you...OR even buy you the Mercedes you want!

Another thing you don't want to do is list stuff like, "blue eyes and blonde hair." Qualifiers like this limit what can MANIFEST. What if the person who was everything you desire had brown eyes? In this situation, that person couldn't show up. On this list, look at what is truly important to you. Look at the life you'd like to have. Is it essential that the person has blue eyes and blonde hair or

a tattoo on their butt? If it is, by all means, ask for it. It is your life to create.

After you've written your desires for both sections, we're going to do something called an "energy pull." To do the energy pull, get the energy of your list, and tap into everyone who will be the items of this list for you. (By simply asking to tap in, you do it. You're doing it already.) Then pull massive amounts of energy from the universe through them and through you until you perceive an expansion in your heart. After you pull enough energy to feel this expansion, trickle energy back out to them so they know it's you who's pulling them when they find you. That's the energy pull, as simple as that. If you don't think you did it or are not sure, you did it! You can do the energy pulls at any time and as often as you would like to. I would recommend doing it at least once a day, or as often as you think to do it.

Now this would be a good place to reiterate...

IT NEVER SHOWS UP THE WAY YOU THINK IT WILL!

After doing this exercise, one morning I woke up while traveling with the intense urge to book a plane ticket to a class that was happening in the next month. It made absolutely no sense, but I booked it. That next month at the class, I met someone. She was wonderful. We hit it off immediately. When I flew back home after the class, we talked on the phone every day. I found my list I had made, and I went "Oh crap! Here she is!" She was everything I had put on my list. At this point many years later I don't remember what I put on it (I don't think I even have the list anymore), but I do remember one thing I put on there:

"Someone who will acknowledge me for the contribution I be."

She was that and is that, and our relationship continues to this day.

By the way, the list doesn't have to be just for pulling in somebody to be in relationship with. It could be for casual sex, friends, a pet, a business partner, a house, or anything else you would like to pull into and create in your life. You can even do it with what you'd like your life to be.

My girlfriend Georgia and I created a list when we were looking for a cat to add to our lives. One of the things we asked for was a cat who wouldn't smell bad. The cat that came to us is the best smelling cat I've ever met. His litter box doesn't even smell, and we keep it in our closet!

Strangely enough, the list also works if you already have somebody you're in a relationship with or married to. When you ask the universe to deliver these different energies to your life, it delivers. You might wake up in the morning to find yourself with a total stranger. They may look like your husband or wife, but they sure as hell aren't acting like they used to! I can't tell you how many people I have heard this from who have used the tools of Access Consciousness.

One last thing...

Let's take one more look at your list. With each item, with everything you desire somebody to be for you, would you please now look at it and ask:

"Would I be willing to be this for me?"

About the Author
Bret Rushia

Bret Rushia has been on a life-long quest to find kindness, sweetness, and laughter. He started using the tools of Access Consciousness while living on his grandparent's couch, at 24, in Long Island New York. Now, four years later, he has a beautiful girlfriend who is also his business partner in a lucrative coaching business, he lives in a downtown high-rise in Houston, TX, and he travels the world attending classes and facilitating on the most important things to him: consciousness, kindness, and self-awareness. Through his work, Bret has facilitated many to see the gift of being them and the gift of discovering the hidden capacities that lie, previously unacknowledged within each of us.

The Relationship Equation

BY ALISON COX

*"I'm not afraid to lose anyone,
and I'll never leave them either." ~ Gary Douglas*

The Relationship Equation

When I was a kid, I learned from Disney movies, children's books, and from my parents that to have a relationship there are three necessary components, much like an equation:

1) A man

2) A woman

3) And a yummy sparkly sprinkling of LOVE.

It seemed like a magical, perfect, delightful combination that if I were lucky enough, someday, I could find someone to enjoy a relationship with. There was someone out there who was absolutely perfect for me: "The One." My soul mate would be someone that, when I found him, would make my life complete.

Who was this going to be? Where would I find him? Was he going to find me? And, if I didn't find him, how was I going to be happy?

Talk about PRESSURE!

My First Love

By age four, the pressure was off.

I had found the love of my life: my dad's friend Tom. He was tall (from my preschool perspective), had a Pontiac Thunderbird, and gave me a Teddy Bear. He was the most "handsomest" man I had ever laid purple-framed glasses covered eyes on.

I had BIG plans for Tom. We were going to be married, play Barbies and Legos all day, eat only Twinkies, and he would, OF COURSE, surprise me with presents at least once hourly.

This relationship seemed like it would last forever. Tom and I really had a connection. We were going to live happily ever after. Tom and I didn't need anyone but each other. Tom and Alison sitting in a tree...K-I-S-S-I-N-G.... Who teaches four-year-olds these songs anyway? Sheesh!

THEN...

The worst day of my impressionable young life happened. Something unfathomable. Something that should not have happened to two people in love. Tom moved to California with some lady named Lori! How could this be? How could he do this to me? This wasn't part of the plan! I was devastated, hurt, and confused. What did Lori have that I didn't?

Was I ever going to be happy? Would I ever find someone as perfect as Tom?

After hours of New Kids On The Block video marathons and a new hamster, I finally calmed down. I lifted my sad little head up and decided to give love another shot. The search continued.... This relationship thing had to be found somewhere!

To pass the time until I discovered the relationship that would make life grand and glorious, I took up hobbies. I loved talking to frogs, torturing my dog, getting sideways ponytails from my dad, playing war with the neighbor boys (and punching them in the gut when they didn't do what I said), building forts, climbing trees, catching bugs, conning my mom into one more hamster (this is the last one I swear), riding my banana seat bike, putting dresses on my brother, and choreographing sweet dance numbers to Paula Abdul songs.

Life was good. Where was Prince Charming to complete the picture?

If at First You, Don't Succeed...

As luck would have it, I fell in love many times...and out of it again.

There was Jamie, who became my boyfriend for a month on the bus home from kindergarten. We had to break up

when he mooned my best friend, Kelly, for no particular reason at all. How rude!

There was Brad Pitt in *Legends of the Fall*, Patrick Swayze from *Dirty Dancing*, and Michelangelo the Ninja Turtle. I had to give up all hopes and dreams of relationships with them—they were a little out of my league, and I didn't know how to reach their publicists.

There was Nick in fourth grade who didn't get that he should love me, even after I broke into his house and threw chocolate kisses all over his kitchen floor. A little thick headed, I'd say!

Ahh, and my first kiss with my best friend's older brother. Doesn't a first kiss constitute a long and loving relationship eventually leading to marriage? Nope...wrong again. I don't think we ever talked again after that!

UGH! What was up with this love thing? This relationship thing? What the hell did being "In Love" mean anyway?

Once again, time had to pass until I found Mr. Right. I enjoyed swimming at the beaches of Lake Michigan, sneaking out with friends, and camping under the stars, secretly drinking my friend's dad's "Natty Lights" in her garage. I also took the opportunity to flirt with every boy in sight, ride the neighbors' horses bareback (we had no idea how to put on a saddle), and to dream about the magical possibilities the future had for me.

Middle school and high school came and went. Still no love. I was beginning to get a little worried. After college, I would SURELY have to have SOME sort of life-long lover lined up! Who was I going to marry? Wasn't that what you did after college? Wasn't it some universal law?

Disney Was Right After All

FINALLY, it happened. The year before I graduated from college, TRUE LOVE finally found me.

Seth was perfect. He was tall, handsome, very funny, and drank a lot. He was artistic, profound, and mysterious, with a splash of life-has-been-hard-and-now-I'm-broken all wrapped into one. All girls love a man who needs fixing, right?

After not even three months of dating and exchanging the "L" word, Seth moved in. Was this real? Was it really true that I got to come home each day to a boy waiting for me? I finally had someone to do mushy things with: someone to hold me, to cook dinner with, to share a glass of wine at the end of the day, and to plot the future adventures we would have. We planned on moving away to Latin America after we both finished college. We even talked about KIDS?! This was serious.

Seth and I loved the same music. We had all the same friends. We liked all the same foods, movies, and bars. We both liked to make weird art. We liked to get drunk and dance like no one was watching. Even our sense of humor was the same.

We were perfect in each other's eyes.

He was a man. I was a woman. We had the yummy sparkling sprinkling of love and then some. BINGO! I had achieved that elusive equation.

Life was panning out accordingly.

No One Tells You How Long Ever After Is...

After nearly a year of what seemed like the best, most magical, most romantic year EVER, things started to shift.

Behaviors that I had never really noticed before began to bug me.

Does he really play that many video games? He has been jobless for how long? Has he always smoked this much pot? Did we really just do the whole, *I'm taking a shower; you're sitting on the toilet, and we're talking about groceries* scenario?

This is what happens to love? I had never felt more alone, out of place, and incomplete in my LIFE!

Seth wasn't exactly having the time of his life either. In fact, he was suffering just as much as I was.

Something had to change.

The Last Straw

"I'm moving to California."

What? Did he really just say that? I had been planning and waiting for all of the exciting plans to unfold. Travel, adventure, and fun—what happened to them? He killed it just like that? I didn't want to go to California and join the weed movement. That wasn't adventure for me!

After the initial blow, I began to ask questions. What now? Where do I go? What is it I really want? What adventure do I want to create?

Something wonderful lit up inside of me. I got an old familiar feeling that I hadn't felt in a long time, the feeling I used to get when I was younger when I was catching frogs, building forts, flirting with boys, and camping under the stars—when I was just being me. At that time, people and places flowed in and out of my life as they liked and I didn't have a point of view about whether I was doing the right thing or not, being the right thing or not, or choosing the right thing or not. It felt like the feeling of total freedom, the feeling of ease and flowing.

This was like a reset button! I didn't have to sit around waiting for someone else to agree with me or give me a hall pass to live. And I didn't have to sit around making another person wrong for what they were choosing either!

That night I looked up a one-way ticket to Honduras and left by mid-summer. I made a promise to myself to always follow that "flying" feeling no matter what. I decided to make myself my number one, to follow what really made me happy in the moment, and to never expect someone else to do or be something they're not.

Relationship Rewrite

Since choosing to change my relationship, I also changed my view of what "relationship" means to me and began to create my new reality in regard to it. By changing the rules of what was supposed to make me happy and creating a new relationship with myself, I have been able to live the adventure of life I always knew was possible. I got to volunteer with children in the jungles of Honduras, swim in the raging currents of wild jungle rivers, teach English to Korean children, taste the sushi in Japan (it tastes totally different than anywhere else on the planet), dance in the full moon parties of Thailand, ride on the backs of camels in the deserts of India, and lead a whole parade of elephants on top of an elephant's head through the forests of Laos. I've created hundreds of relationships with men, women, places, and animals all over the world.

I was able to be and choose what really makes me happy, and I continue to do so to this day.

What if your relationship with yourself was the most generative and gratifying relationship you had? That doesn't mean others don't still come (or go), but when you make your relationship with yourself your greatest priority, you always give yourself everything you were expecting, hoping, and praying to get from someone else. What if you could be the source of having everything you ever dreamed of?

What if it's the adventure of creating a life that works for you and what if life were a constant, never-ending stream of new experiences, new relationships, new beginnings? And what can you receive from the "endings"? What do you do when it's over?

When something ends, does it really end? When you have a breakup, or someone dies, or you have to move, do you get sad and dwell? Or do you choose to see and receive the gift that person/place/thing was to you at the time? What if you can continue to receive from it after that? What if everything "lost" is just a possibility for something greater to show up that wouldn't have been possible had you not had that person or experience in the first place?

What if "relationship" isn't about finding "The One" or finding someone to complete you? The people you connect with or separate from are not what give you value. They never have been and never will be. What if YOU complete you? What if the people, places, and actions you include in your life are just there to amplify who you BE?

Discovering that being in a relationship does not mean I have to be caged, caught, or stunted is thrilling and opens up a whole new world of possibilities I didn't even know were possible. I don't have to limit myself or live up or down to anyone else's standards. Now my reality with relationship is more like, "Who or what is fun to play with today?"

I don't know about you, but to me that sounds EXCITING!

I can have more than one relationship—not enjoying anything or anyone "exclusively" but enjoying all of it. My happiness and self-worth does not rely on one person, but on choosing to have gratitude for everything and everyone in my life, including me. WOW! More of that, please!

Beyond The Equation

Finding a relationship is not going to happen by following any kind of pre-calculated, "one size fits all" equation. What works for one person may not for another. There is no status quo. The equation is what you make it. Relationship can and will be as exciting and adventurous as you make it. It can be as boring and torturous as you'd like to make it as well. There is no right or wrong, just, what kind of life would you like to have? What kind of relationships would you like to create? Again, who or what is going to be fun to play with? And if it doesn't work, are you willing to change it?

I'd like to propose a new equation, one that doesn't have a fixed or correct answer. Instead of the old "man + woman + love = relationship," what if the new relationship equation could be something like:

You + What's fun for you + Action = A Relationship Beyond

"A relationship beyond" can mean greater possibilities, more choice, adventure, joy, gratitude, happiness and more of whatever you are willing to ask for.

Who or what are you willing to ask for that you haven't asked for yet?

What adventures would you like to have that you haven't chosen yet?

Who or what have you overlooked, that if you acknowledged the gift he, she, or it was, would allow more possibilities to show up than you ever could have imagined?

I've committed and demanded of myself to ask these questions every day and all I can say is...HOLY SHIT! The relationships I'm cultivating with old friends, new friends, lovers, family, money, work, the planet, and (most importantly) with myself are truly magical and more phenomenal than anything I have ever experienced before.

Try it! What have you got to lose? You just might create a life full of beautiful, ever changing and growing relationships and experiences that keep getting better, greater, and BEYOND what anyone has told you is possible!

About the Author

Alison Cox

Alison Cox is a master at facilitating people into greater possibilities. Whether they are seeking to have more ease with their bodies, looking to step into happier relationships with their partners, asking to generate greater income, or seeking communion with the planet, Alison is excited to catalyze those changes.

Growing up in a small town in Michigan, Alison could never understand all the rules she was told she had to follow. She knew there had to be more to life, so when she was old enough she embarked on a journey that took her from Asia to Latin America to Europe and beyond. In each place she fell in love with the land, the animals, the food, and the people.

Where she thought she was looking for a place to belong, Alison discovered that she was actually seeking the adventure of being the person she truly is *everywhere* she goes and with *everyone* she meets.

She now aims to share her discoveries and concepts with anyone also seeking a life and living that works for them by empowering others using dynamic tools, questions, and clearings to create a reality they have always known is possible.

Alison Cox is an Access Consciousness® Certified Facilitator, Talk the the Entities™ Facilitator, Best Friend to Maggie the Hound Dog, Bodyworker extraordinaire, and Founder and Creator of Alivio Massage Therapy in Denver, Colorado. She may be contacted at AlisonCoxCFMW@gmail.com or https://www.facebook.com/AlisonCoxCFMW/ for more information on classes, events, and private facilitation or bodywork sessions.

Traveling the 7 Cs:

7 COMPONENTS TO GENERATING, CREATING, AND SUSTAINING CONSCIOUS RELATIONSHIPS

BY DR. SARAH BROTSKY

When I sat down to write this chapter, I was instantly flooded with a slew of ideas that I knew desired to be included and shared. The chapter was screaming out to be written. Well, ok, maybe just yelling to be heard? Let's face it, unconscious relationships on planet earth tend to be highly dysfunctional, relentlessly stressful, and anything but easy! And this dysfunction is certainly not exclusive to intimate relationships. Unconsciousness pervades relationships with family members, friends, bosses, and co-workers, bringing challenges and utter confusion... It even permeates relationship to self!

Why is that, you may ask? Unconscious relationships often come from a "fairy tale" point of view, a "one day my prince or princess will come" mentality that results in unrealistic expectations, disappointments, incompleteness, and dissatisfaction. These attitudes lead to an outward journey, an endless search to try to find the right person, or the "right ONE" to complete oneself. This ineffective search often backfires and creates feelings of frustration, exhaustion, and confusion. To add some more trauma and drama to the mix, a needy, self-sacrificing dependency tends to kick in, leading the way to resentment, anger, and sadness... possibly even a rebellion against the relationship structure itself. Not exactly the lightest way to live!

So what keeps us repeating and returning to these types of relationships again and again? What drives us to continue to do the same thing over and over and still think, "Next time, I'll get it right."? Isn't that the definition of insanity?! And how is it that what we deem to be so magnificent, beautiful, and everlasting often ends in a whirlwind of devastation? Then we top it off by berating ourselves and/or blaming the other person, assuming it MUST be someone's fault. It's nonsensical craziness! Even the most ultra-analytical human is bound to be confused. We are creatures of habit and living unconsciously amplifies that. How's that working for us?

Are there other possibilities?

There must be some alternative route.... Is there another choice? There is. It's called living consciously!

Gary Douglas, Founder of Access Consciousness®, describes consciousness as "the ability to be present in your life in every moment, without judgment of you or anyone else. It is the ability to receive everything, reject nothing, and create everything you desire in life—greater than what you currently have, and more than what you can imagine."

What then, is a conscious relationship?

A conscious relationship is one that functions from a space of awareness, allowance, possibility, and choice. It is a space in which each Being is authentically himself or herself, without the need to cut off awareness, points of view, or preferences in order to satisfy the other. A conscious relationship welcomes in a higher form of communication, one that aids in getting clear on what is present and desired. The space created tends to be generative and expansive, and allows growth and change to occur in an unimpeded way.

Aye, aye, captain.
A conscious relationship to self?

What if I told you that you are the captain of your life? What if you are much greater than you perceive yourself to be and more capable than you give yourself credit for? You have an internal compass of sorts, one that allows you to be and perceive the truth of what is. What if you are your own reference to creating your own points of view?

Accessing your compass is simply about tapping into your awareness. Using your mind to figure things out by weighing right or wrong and taking all known variables into consideration can be time intensive and challenging. When you become aware of the energy of light and heavy, and use that to choose and decide, you can make your choices from a space of awareness, which is far easier than mulling things over with your mind. The idea of light and heavy refers to the energy or "charge" you perceive when you ask a question. It allows you to reside in your awareness, or "knowing."

An invitation to something greater.

I now invite you on a journey with me into the "7 C's." These C's—Clear, Choice, Caring, Contribution, Change, Creating, and Connection—are a key to generating and sustaining conscious relationships. With the Conscious Relationship Compass© as our guide, we will take a non-linear approach to discovering and navigating the relationships already in your life and those you desire to create.

As we explore this tool that I'm sharing with you, remember there is no right or wrong to it, and certainly no "supposed to's"! Simply be present and tune into your knowing, awareness, and points of view. Ask questions, and trust what you know. Are you ready to set sail and merge into something so new and different that it could create a world of undiscovered possibilities? Ok, let's get started!

Conscious Relationship Compass©

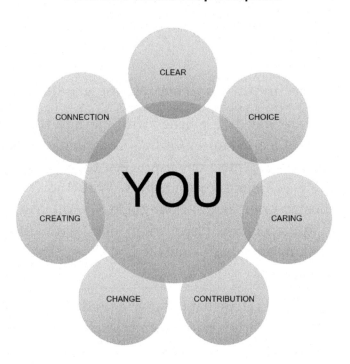

Let the Conscious Relationship Compass© be your guide.

The Conscious Relationship Compass© serves as a pragmatic and systematic tool that allows you to see if your current relationships are functioning from a conscious space. Not only does it assist in generating greater awareness regarding existing relationships, but it also allows for the possibility of creating new, sustainable ones with ease.

Conscious Relationship Compass©

The Conscious Relationship Compass© is easy to use. Start by bringing into your awareness a relationship you would like to focus on; either one that already exists or one you would like to create. Next, read through all of the "7 C Descriptions." Then go to the "Explorative Questions," to ask yourself each of the questions and be present with the energy with which it resonates. If you get a light, expansive energy on all the 7 C's, it's likely your relationship is already functioning consciously. If any of the C's are dense or heavy, explore the additional questions.

The 7 C Descriptions:

Clear: easy to perceive, understand, or interpret. When you are clear, you access your awareness, allowance, perceiving, knowing, and receiving and there's a void of thoughts, feelings, and emotions (or lower frequency, black-and-white thinking). For a relationship to be conscious, it is important to GET CLEAR on all aspects of the relationship—what you would like it to be like as well as what you would like it not to be like.

Choice: the act of selecting a possibility by using your knowing (a "light" or "heavy" energy). Choice creates awareness and opens the door to other possibilities. When it comes to a relationship, particularly a conscious one, choosing to be in it is essential to sustaining it.

Caring: a display of kindness and gratitude; a loving space with no conditions or judgments. Caring for another in a conscious way invites deeper connection, more allowance, and greater possibilities.

Contribution: a gift; a state of simultaneous giving and receiving. In a conscious relationship, contribution is a two-way path that fosters greater creation and accomplishments.

Creating: energy that is used to actualize something into existence. It is easy to see how this applies to new conscious relationships. The energy of creating in any relationship, new or old, enables the relationship to remain generative and sustainable.

Change: choosing something different in order to create a different result. In conscious relationships, it is about being willing to be in the ebb and flow of life and remaining open to the possibility of choosing differently if something is not working.

Connection: an energy shared between two Beings. This energy allows both to tap into something greater. It is a space where open communication (a sharing of information in a way the other being can receive it) is available and points of view are acknowledged without having to validate or invalidate the other person's position: a place free from the restraints of inhibitions.

Explorative Questions

The questions below are aimed to stimulate awareness and do not require any definitive answers.

Are the 7 C's in my relationship light or heavy?

If light, your relationship is likely already functioning in a conscious way. Congratulations!

If heavy, let's take a look at where it can be transformed:

Which of the 7 C's are heavy?

Take them one at a time and ask:

- ★ Would I like to change it?

- ★ Can it be changed?

- ★ How do I change it?

- ★ What is possible here that I haven't considered?

- ★ What other questions can I ask that would bring greater awareness?

Go through this process with each C that has a density to it until you have an awareness of what you can change about your relationship to make it more conscious.

Example:

Here's a brief example of one of my clients navigating "Contribution," one of the 7 C's she identified as heavy in the relationship with her boyfriend. She asked herself the questions from the Conscious Relationship Compass© and this is a snapshot of what she discovered:

★ Would I like to change it?

Yes

★ Can it be changed?

Yes

★ How do I change it?

By being more aware and open to receiving mutual exchanges of intimacy and vulnerability.

Communicate this newfound awareness to my boyfriend.

★ What is possible here that I haven't considered?

Areas in our relationship where contribution is working.

★ What other questions can I ask that would bring greater awareness?

What is my boyfriend's point of view on contribution?

Where have I cut myself off from receiving?

What would it take to create something greater together?

What now?

With the awareness you received from the Conscious Relationship Compass©, you can now identify some new possibilities that if chosen, would aid in generating, creating, and sustaining something different in your life.

So first take one of the possibilities and ask, "If I choose this (fill in the blank) will it contribute to my life six months from now? What will it contribute to my life six years from now?" Feeling a sensation of ease or lightness means "yes" and that choice if chosen, would contribute to a greater future. If you get a feeling of contraction, or "no," ask, "What else could I choose? What other possibilities are there?" Keep exploring until you discover a "light" possibility. This process will bring more clarity about what will and will not contribute to your relationship, allowing it to function from a more conscious space.

Un-final words...

When you are aware, following your knowing, and living in the space where you can readily choose something different, what does that create? Conscious relationships! How does it get any better? Did you know that it takes only one conscious Being to generate a conscious relationship? Would you be willing to be that person? What other possibilities would that create? What change would be possible if you chose that? And what if you BEing you is the difference your life, your relationships, and the world require? Let the journey continue!

I hope this chapter has provided you with some tools that assist you in generating, creating, and sustaining conscious relationships. Use it. Live it. Be it. The possibilities are endless!

About the Author
Dr. Sarah Brotsky

Dr. Sarah Brotsky is a clinical psychologist who has been in private practice for over 16 years. She has been on both national television and radio programs as an authority on a variety of psychological topics and has been published in an international journal as well as has written for a number of different publications.

Dr. Sarah's approach centers around empowering people to tap into their own conscious way of being and to encourage them to live from a space that allows them to change through choice.

Along with her clinical skills and training as a psychologist, Dr. Sarah uses Access Consciousness® tools in her private practice to help clients clear anything that does not contribute to their overall wellbeing. By actively using these tools in her life, Dr. Sarah serves as an example of the benefits that living consciously can generate and actualize. This has allowed for greater possibilities in healing and a higher therapeutic success rate when it comes to treating anxiety, depression, and a variety of mental health concerns. Dr. Sarah is also an Access Consciousness® Certified Facilitator.

If you would like to reach Dr. Sarah, you can contact her at drsarahbrotsky@gmail.com.

Visit her website at www.drsarahbrotsky.com.

You can also connect with her on:

Facebook:
https://www.facebook.com/drsarahbrotsky/

Instagram:
https://www.instagram.com/drsarahbrotsky/

Saying Yes

BY JENNIFER CRAMER LEWIS

I am thrilled and honoured to connect with you on my favourite topic! My work with people and their relationships is extremely valuable to me, and I believe that when we are in a soulmate partnership, all of our horizons are infinitely enhanced. We improve not only our life and the life of our partner but also the lives of our children, family members, clients, community, and ultimately the world.

I am sure that you are no stranger to the statistics on divorce, but here they are: in Canada, where I live, just over 400 out of 1000 marriages end in divorce each year. The average age for those getting divorced hovers around 44 for Men and 41 for Women.

Does that alarm you or cause some trepidation? You are not alone!

My ex-husband and I were very much in love when we got married. In fact, we were so head over heels that we only dated for six months before the big day. Things changed when we had children. The stress of having two kids under two years of age was too much for us; we were not one of those couples that got stronger with the test of time. I remember specifically two incidents; the first was when I stood outside of myself and watched how my husband talked to me in front of our boys and just knew that I couldn't be that person anymore. I had to leave.

The other defining moment was seven years later. One night I came home to an empty house again, and thought to myself, "Boy, it sure would be nice to have someone to curl up on the couch with tonight!" Then I immediately thought to myself, "So, they can talk about themselves for two hours and then want sexual favors?"

With an attitude like that, I was surely not attracting phenomenal men into my life. No wonder I was alone for seven years after breaking up with my husband.

Instead of beating myself up over my feelings, I questioned them. If I had a bad attitude about having a soulmate in my life, what could change that energy? What could I do to change how I look at marriage and what I believe about being in a loving relationship? I was given the advice that to be a loving partner to someone else, you have to have the practice of loving yourself. This sent me on a search, looking for what made me happy and what made me feel loved in the world.

Now that I am in a loving soulmate relationship, I am committed to showing my students and clients that a loving

7

relationship is a real possibility for them and that anyone can choose a partner who is a contribution to every area of their life. Would you like to have someone who "gets" you, someone who always has your back, who knows what you like and loves to please you? My partner has those qualities and yours can too.

No matter how scared you are, or how long it has been since you were in a relationship, you can start to change your energy, your frequency, and your ability to attract that special person.

To change my energy, I went on a search for information. I began to meditate on a regular basis. I took some courses online and eventually cobbled together my own program to assist me with the changes I had chosen to make. I am a lifelong learner and believe strongly in the power of having a coach to assist me, but I found nothing holistic that involved not only cognitive and behaviour changes but also incorporated the body.

I was willing to make an investment of both time and money to discover the missing links to what I always knew was possible and hadn't yet been able to accomplish.

Intuitively I must have known that I was going to share my message. I journaled, made lists and documented everything that I did to change my frequency and attract my soulmate. I also noted everything that I have done to improve my relationship skills, including the tools we rely on to have a supportive, thriving relationship to this day.

Now that I am in this loving partnership, I am living a life that is beyond anything I thought possible only a few years ago. We go on adventures together to India, Guatemala, and Costa Rica and on road trips to Victoria, Seattle, and Kelowna. We love art and have collected some gorgeous pieces to decorate our home. Tom was committed to me feeling at home in his space and encouraged me to redecorate so it was reflective of us as a couple. If you really want to get to know someone, renovate a house together. Or don't.

My real mission is for regular people to have everything they need to create a loving soulmate partnership. If they don't have one right now, great! If they already have a partner and it's not that loving, great! Wherever you start, that's just your starting point. The sky isn't even the limit for you!

I have a friend who married a man who everyone thought was Prince Charming. Six foot two, eyes of blue...fun, sexy, charming, and handsome; he even owned a lucrative business. For several years, things were marvelous. They went on trips; he paid for her to go to university and everything was just great. Then he went through a rough time and wasn't able to turn back. He became verbally abusive to her and she didn't know what she should do. From the outside looking in, it seemed that they had it all, but on the inside something was rotten. His bad patch cost them tens of thousands of dollars in his attempts to make himself feel better. In hindsight, she stayed longer than she thought she should have. After she finally left, it didn't take her long to find an amazing man that is so much better suited to her and adds to every area of her life.

While assisting my friend with this breakup, I realized how committed I am to helping people choose relationships that work for them. What would it be like if you had a partner who was fun? What would it be like if you knew you were the fun one? My friend was a great, loving, fun, sexy partner, but she was not in a relationship that allowed her to shine.

Do you have a point of view that if people knew the true you, they wouldn't like you? Ready to blow that up?

I am excited to share five of the things that had a profound influence on my attitude and how I was showing up in the world! I hope you will experiment and see what feels right for you.

The first thing I did was write a list of all the qualities that I loved in a partner and all the things that were non-negotiables. Whenever I look back, I continue to be thrilled and amazed as to how it showed up. Tom is everything that I asked for, and he didn't have any of the qualities that definitely would not work for me. Making a list invites the universe to start creating opportunities *with* you. Do you have a point of view that if you ask for something, it can't show up? The opposite is true...the more we ask for, the more the universe will provide. Remember "Ask and ye shall receive?" They put that in the Bible so we couldn't find out that it is the universal truth that rules all possibilities.... If you don't ask for what you love, you run the risk of not getting it.

I began meditating twice daily on having a soulmate partner. What would that feel like for my body? What would we do together? What would he smell like? Really! The more detail you put into your meditation about what you would like your partner to be like, the better. When I met Tom and as I got to know him, I was delighted again and again by his similarities to my meditations.

Next, I started to clean out my physical and mental space. I went through every part of my physical space and asked if each item matched the frequency of what I was creating. I opened every drawer and looked at every belonging. I purged the clothes and jewelry that didn't match how I wanted to feel and express myself in the world. I was ruthless! If it didn't match, I sold it, gave it away, or recycled it. I also got rid of everything that had been given to me by another man. I will admit, some of it was tough. But in the end, it was totally worth it. I created room in my home, closets, and bedroom for the new life I was creating. My energetic space was open and had room for a soulmate to come in.

The third thing I did was make a list of all the things that I loved doing, like singing and dancing; road trips and vacations; cooking and having guests over; hiking in the forest and going to the ocean and climbing on the rocks; trying new restaurants and learning new things. Then I started doing these activities by myself or with friends. I didn't wait for someone to take me on a date. I took myself, regularly. This was the practice of loving me, taking care of me, and entertaining me that I now show my clients and students.

The fourth thing I did was to create a vision board with images of everything I love to do. Instead of a static vision board, I created a movie with pictures, words, and music. Watching it brought a sense of enjoyment of being with my partner and loving my life. I love this video and still watch it now and again to remind myself of the magic I am capable of creating. I even show it to my students to inspire them to ask the universe to assist them in creating their lives. My inspiration for the vision board came from a scientific study I read showing that the brain cannot tell the difference between fact or fiction if it receives evocative images in combination with music that stimulate an emotional response in the body. Watching the movie each morning and evening allowed me to visit my future life and quickly change my frequency from frustration and loneliness to joy and anticipation.

Finally, I started to say yes to everything I was offered. Instead of saying no, or "I'll think about it," I just said yes. It was this daily meditation of saying yes that led me to so many more expansive and FUN opportunities, including meeting my partner Tom.

One of the funniest aspects of meeting my soulmate partner was how he showed up. I had tried online dating, and it didn't suit me. It seemed so much like catalogue shopping—there was always someone better looking on the next page. This seemed so out of touch. One day, out of the blue, my boss asked if I was interested in going on a blind date. I said yes, and made arrangements to meet at a local restaurant. When I met Tom, he was quiet, well dressed, well groomed and he smelled good. A great start! As we began to date, I called him "Mr. Good on Paper." He had a career, was well respected, did volunteer work, had fitness goals (and was pursuing them) and was generous with his time and his money. He always asked me out on another date at the end of the date we were on. How kind is that? None of that drama, "Will he call or won't he?"

As we began to date more seriously, I had worries that we might fall into patterns and become inauthentic with each other. This strengthened my determination to be 100% myself no matter what, and to check in to see if Tom was too. We began to create a way of being together that centered on being happy. Doing things together that are joyful to both of us has formed a sustainable way of living. So many couples have a honeymoon phase in which they are so bent on impressing each other that they forget about what they actually like to do in favour of pleasing the other person. We did not go there!

One of the things we have learned is to have our "big talks" naked in bed together. If one of us needs to cry, or if we need to explore something uncomfortable, we do it together in a place where we feel safe and vulnerable at the same time. Putting up energetic barriers does not often happen at our house. When it does, we know that it is time to talk and ask questions so we can clear them out.

Another thing that we have learned is not to give up and never quit the relationship, by choosing to be present and look at it with a beginner's mind daily. "Who is my partner today, and how much fun can we have together?" is one of the questions I start my day with. Never giving up and never quitting allows the soulmate partnership to grow and change with the support that it requires from time to time.

The biggest thing that I would love to leave you with is a sense that no matter where you are right now, a loving soulmate partner who is compatible, fun, and sexy is out there for you. The possibilities are infinite for creating this in your universe. Even if you just do the steps outlined in this chapter, the universe is working to make sure that you meet the people you need to meet in order to have your soulmate show up.

Please just say "Yes!"

About the Author
Jennifer Cramer Lewis

Jennifer came to this planet with an inner knowing of how people work and a laser-sharp ability to draw lines between what people were saying, what they were doing, and what they were hoping to accomplish. Jennifer started speaking at four months of age and quickly after that, ideas about what people could do differently would pop into her head and out her mouth they would fly!

Telling adults what they were doing wrong and what they could do to improve their lives wasn't popular; Jennifer was often in trouble for sharing her findings.

Jennifer learned to read at age three. She loved using new words and reading giant books. Luckily, her Mom was excited by her thirst for knowledge and bought her new books regularly. Jennifer combed the house for anything exciting to read and found not only novels and *National Geographic* magazines, but also the Dictionary, the Bible, *The Way,* and *Collier's Encyclopedia.* In reading, she found an entertaining friend to nourish her famished curiosity about people.

Jennifer started attending self-development courses at sixteen. When the people in her class discovered that she was not an adult, they were surprised and annoyed that she had insight beyond her years. She interpreted this attitude to mean that she was too candid, too blunt, too helpful, and that it was somehow all too much for the world around her. For many years, she dialed it back, dulled it down and tried to stuff herself into the box that everyone around her seemed to fit into so stylishly.

In early adulthood, Jennifer discovered a capacity for real estate and in turn, sold, financed, and managed residential, commercial and investment properties. She worked in this field for the majority of her adult life, using her capacities to change some of the processes for financing and managing real estate so that the people who lived there could enjoy their homes more and have the real estate gain value, so it did!

In 2010, at a very low point in her life, Jennifer discovered Access Consciousness® while listening to an internet radio show. Hearing a facilitator explain that 98 percent of our thoughts and feelings are not even ours, Jennifer had a lightbulb moment. Perhaps she wasn't too much; perhaps she really didn't want to exit the planet; she was just more aware of the thoughts and feelings of the people around her than the average person.

So excited about this new knowledge and the new ease in her body, she jumped right in and got her Access Consciousness Bars® Facilitator license. Soon thereafter, she became an Access Consciousness Certified Facilitator as well as an Access Body Process Facilitator.

Helping people become more aware of what they know about their lives is Jennifer's full-time job, and she couldn't be happier. Her clients laugh out loud when things fly out of her mouth that they have been thinking or feeling for years!

Jennifer's biggest hope for her clients is that they stop looking to the past to create their future and that she can be a catalyst for them to create the life that they always knew was possible and didn't know how to initiate. Jennifer loves when her clients learn to laugh again. Her true superpower is combining facilitation with a sense of humour that allows participants to drop years of self-judgement off at the curb.

Every day, Jennifer asks, "How did I get so lucky?" because she is thrilled with the changes that she has made to her everyday life with the tools of Access Consciousness. These include the actualization of an amazing, sexy, soulmate partnership and fulfillment of her fantasy wedding to her husband, Tom.

If you have discovered a burning desire for change in your life and living, Jennifer is available worldwide for group and private coaching programs with both individuals and corporations. She loves to facilitate Access Consciousness Foundation Classes, Bars and Body Classes, Right Relationship for You™ New Beginnings as well as her specialty classes like "Soulmate Blueprint" and "How to Grow Your Business without Blowing You Up." Contact Jennifer on her website, www.brillianceblueprint.ca and she invites you to connect with her on Facebook at Jennifer Cramer Lewis.

Choosing for You and Styling a Relationship that Works for You

By Kass Thomas

We sometimes think we have no options in a relationship. We think we have only one choice and we have a lot of reasons and justifications as to why this is our only choice; I have to stay in this relationship, *because, because, because, because*....

When I went to India for the first time, I did several private sessions with women who felt bound to relationships that weren't working for them. Their reasons were always the same: due to their financial situation, with no money of their own, they had to stay in their relationship because their husbands had control of the bank accounts; their parents were invested in them staying in the relationship;

and the children, always the children. That was their point of view.

My friend Dain Heer once said, "It is our point of view that creates our reality," and the more I travel, the more I find this to be true. If we feel trapped in a relationship, we *feel* like we're in jail. But the reality is we are not in jail, we simply have a point of view about the relationship that does not allow us to feel the freedom that is possible for us.

What point of view do you have that's creating your reality?

Once you realize that you can change your point of view about your partner, about your marriage, or about your life, you see how easy it is to have choice, no matter what the situation is. Just by looking at something from a different point of view, a new perspective, a different angle, you change that situation and your reality.

How many people are trying desperately to break through walls or force open a door so they can get out of something or go beyond a limitation? Often once they break down that wall, they realize they were already beyond their perceived limitation. We all have infinite choices, but as long as we're functioning from a "no choice" reality, we don't feel capable of choosing something greater than what we see in front of us: the wall, the closed door, the jail.

What "no choice" reality are you creating?

Many of us choose relationships totally based on societal beliefs; I know I did. My first husband was "the typical right choice." He was educated, from a good family, creative, had a good job, handsome, 6ft 2in, artistic, spiritual, and engaging. He was older than I (fourteen years older) with all the right stuff to fit into this reality perfectly. I said, "Ok, this part is easy. I'll marry him. Check." And I checked off marriage on my laundry list of tasks that would allow me to be normal, real and the same as everyone else.

I envisioned having my 2.5 kids and comfortably fitting into the upper middle-class echelon of intellectual America. A bit political (not too much), and international (we both spoke French, and loved to travel and eat different ethnic foods), we were slightly everything and not too much of anything. Perfect! I was 22 years old, had just graduated, and had a great job which gave us access to the best restaurants in New York City, as well as free tickets to theater, fabulous gifts at Christmas from clients, and lots of travel. The illusion had begun!

About ten years into the marriage, my whole life turned upside down. Maybe it happened even earlier, but that is when I realized it. It started with a series of events over a six-month period that forced me to look at what I had been ignoring, thanks to all the perks of the "perfect life."

First, one of my very best friends was dying. Instead of following my heart, choosing for me, and staying home to comfort my friend in his last days, I succumbed to relationship pressures and went away on vacation with my husband. My friend died while I was away and it devastated me. Upon returning to New York, in addition to dealing with the loss of my friend, I also lost my job of eight years, and my relationship was all but over.

In an attempt to seek normalcy and return to some kind of balance, I put the word out that I was available for hire and was immediately offered a similar position in a better company. I remember being at the bus stop ready to get on the bus and I somehow could not bring myself to go on the interview. The interview was purely a formality; the job was mine. Still, I found myself paralyzed and unable to get on the bus. Something had shifted, things were changing. I knew the universe was giving me a chance to really step up and make a change in my life, and if I went on that interview, I would simply be switching one "perfect and real and normal life" for another. It was over, now what?

So instead of taking a stable, good paying job in a career I had built up for almost ten years, I went on unemployment for the first time in my life. My husband went crazy. I had been the steady breadwinner in the family at that point, and this was not comfortable. While trying to figure out where, who, what, and why I was, I got an offer to start traveling as a tour manager with a dear friend. She was just starting her singing career, and while she couldn't pay me a salary, she could pay for my flights, lodging, and meals. "Perfect," she said, "while you are figuring out what you want to do, come use your skills to organize my travel and act as interpreter for me." Our first tour was to Europe, where I had lived for a year about a decade prior, before my marriage, before my job, before the "perfect and normal life" choices.

On that trip, I began to recognize a familiar vibration, the vibration of who I was before my relationship. When the fairytale dust blew away, along with it went the hue of the illusion that *this is the perfect partner, and now I will finally live "normal" like everyone else.* I saw my reality and that there were so many things I wasn't enjoying, so many parts of me had not been living, being, expressing, in order to accommodate the lifestyle and relationship.

Breaking through the fog called your life

When I lost my job, I started a home-study book called *The Artist's Way*. It involves doing eight weeks of morning writing—stream of consciousness—and not reading it until the time period is complete. After the eight weeks, when I went back and read what I had written, I was so embarrassed; I had basically written the same thing every morning and never realized it. Each morning, as if it were the first time, I would write about how miserable I was in my relationship. It was such a shock to me because I had no idea that I was writing the same thing every morning, no idea how truly miserable I was, no idea about how much of me I had cut off to accommodate the relationship.

Isn't it interesting that when we're not willing to see something, no matter how obvious it is, we just don't see it? It obviously was not the right life for me or the right relationship for me; the coordinates were not mine, they were a set of coordinates dictated by this reality, and somehow I bought them hook, line and sinker. Sink her.

When we do that, when we are not choosing and styling our relationship to fit who we are, we don't see where we are cutting off awareness. We don't see all those parts of us that are not showing up anymore because we have turned off the lights on that area of our lives. No air time. For me, the period of six months that included the death of my friend, the loss of my job, and finally the end of my relationship, changed my life completely and changed the way I choose and create all my relationships today.

Choosing life; choosing to live for me

Any relationship that ends is like a death of sorts. When you enter into a relationship with another person, the relationship takes on a life force of its own. There's you, the other person, and what you two create together. It's like a project. You may call it a friendship, a marriage, or even a partnership with a colleague, or a group or business, it's your rapport with the person or entity that constitutes your relationship. You in relation to them equals your relationship. When it ends or transforms, you go through a period of change which can sometimes be uncomfortable for you and for others. Everything has to adjust, as it has an effect on everyone and everything around you, whether they choose to recognize it or not. That too is a choice.

Part of the change that showed up for me after my first marriage was that I began to realize, all my life I had always been trying to make everyone else happy. I was the eternal peacemaker, even as a child. I never desired to stir things up, and never purposely desired to draw attention to myself; I was always thinking about others. Looking back, that is pretty funny since I was everything but a neutral presence. I did my best to keep the peace and soothe the seas of conflict in the lives of my family and friends, and anywhere else I could.

After my breakup, that changed a bit. I changed a bit. I began looking at all aspects of my life, questioning everything, and choosing to honor what was going on inside of me in any given moment, instead of living my life from the point of view of making others happy. This was not easy for the people around me. They had become very comfortable with our relationships as they were, and they were not ready for that to change just because my life as I knew it had fallen apart. I remember being on the phone with my mother and sister shortly after my break up, and not playing "my normal role," I wasn't the person they were used to. I remember them saying I sounded a little cranky, to which I responded, "My whole life has changed. My whole life. Forgive me if I'm a little different! I think I have the right!"

Ah! Finally, I could say it. Instead of bending and folding to accommodate what they required, with the excuse of the breakup, the loss of my job, the death of my friend, I was finally willing to say, "You know what? This is what is showing up for me right now. I am honoring that, and I am really sorry if it doesn't please you at the moment. This is what I require." It felt good.

I recognized that in my first marriage, I had never clearly stated when things did not work for me. Always the peacemaker, I was the one ready to change and adapt me to try to get things to work out. There comes a point at which you have to take stock and recognize which things are not working and assess what needs to change in order to move forward. In the beginning, this "choice for me" seemed to be a choice against everyone else, or at least that is the way they took it. They didn't realize and neither did I, that a change in your point of view can change the way you approach transformation and make it easier for everyone.

In fact, my first husband was quite surprised when, after a long conversation in which we both agreed on an extensive list of things that were not working in our relationship, I suggested we break up. What!?! It is amazing how people are willing to stay in a relationship that is not working and have no desire or impetus to change it. They don't realize you can change your relationship by changing what isn't working: "Look, this doesn't work for me.... This is a deal breaker; either it changes, or I am gone."

Somehow, I felt that as the product of both my parents' second marriages (they both already had children when I came along, and I was the only child of this new marriage) I absolutely knew that divorce was something I didn't want to do. They got together while they were both in other relationships, so I knew that being unfaithful was also something I was unwilling to do. In choosing a relationship I think that's what a lot of people do—enter relationships based on everything they know they don't want. It doesn't have this, this, and this, therefore I'm choosing it, rather than, "What do I desire?" It's a half empty version of life. What's there and can I deal with it?

I started asking some questions about what kind of relationship would work for me, what I really desired in a relationship, and what would not work for me.

After asking these questions for about a year and a half, avoiding any serious relationships, and choosing for me, a guy whom I had met years prior when I lived in Europe came to New York for a wedding, and he called me. I wasn't looking for a relationship, and neither was he, so we had a lovely platonic, yet romantic time in New York. I often traveled to Europe on my tour manager job, and this allowed us to continue our romantic but noncommittal dance for about a year. At that point, the music changed, the dance sped up, and I eventually moved to Rome to be with him and start a new life. It felt really light—no bending and changing me to make it work. I knew it was the beginning of another chapter and shortly thereafter, a new marriage.

When I started this new relationship, I had decided that I would do it completely different from my previous one. I did the opposite of what I had done with my ex—I was very vocal about everything. I would tell him when things didn't work. "Wrong toothpaste! That's not going to work for me!" or "No music in the house; that doesn't work for me."

I remember going with him to a party at a client's house. When we got there, my new guy didn't introduce me around as his girlfriend. "That doesn't work for me!" I told him. He responded by saying, "I've never been in a relationship like this before. If it's what you require, I'm happy to introduce you. I never introduce anybody, but if that's what you need, I'll do it." His caring response diffused all my defensive posture.

One of the things I realized in those early days is how many people are walking around with a chip on their shoulder waiting for someone to step out of line so they can unleash their anger. I had gone from the peacemaker in my relationships to an explosion waiting to happen. *Make my day. Say something so I can release my pent up frustrations on you.* Having lived in New York, I had a lot of that attitude. Every time I said, "That doesn't work for me," my new partner would respond, with complete calm, "OK, I can change that, no problem. I didn't know that was important to you. It won't happen again." And it never did. Simple. Easy. What if a choice for us does not have to be a choice against someone else? What if we could simply state what works for us and allow the other person to choose it or not?

While some people have the "make my day" posture, others play the peacemaker, as I did in my early days. The desire to keep the peace at all costs by avoiding conflict or disagreement is the opposite side of the coin from unleashing your anger. In both cases, your life and relationship are based on solving problems instead of creating something together, something different that may not exist yet. When you create your life based on what you don't want, your position is about excluding and eliminating things that don't work for you rather than choosing what would work for you and being willing to have someone choose to accommodate that or not. Either way, this posture is not a choice against them, simply a choice for you.

What else is possible in relationships? What about kindness?

My husband and I have been together 20 years now, and this is a snapshot of how our relationship works. We're really clear about what doesn't work so we can change it. It was interesting for me to ask early on, "What doesn't work for you?" His response was, "Dishes all over the counter... piled in the sink is fine, just not all over the counter." I was shocked. "WHAT!?!? That's it?" Yup!

"I don't need you to clean. I don't need you to cook, I'm a great cook. I don't need any of that from you." Wow! I was so relieved about that. Even as a young college kid, if

I had ten dollars, five of it would go to have someone clean the house. Even if it meant I didn't eat for a couple days, at least I'd have a clean house. (I was skinnier back then!) This helped me realize that it's really about me being me in relationship. I was the valuable product for him. Me. That was very new for me and quite delightful.

So many of us go through relationships with roles. There's some part of the deal and deliver in a relationship that one person does the planning, the other earns the money, or takes care of the house, or whatever it is you are "responsible for." When it's about you, and exploring who you are, it brings a level of freedom and discovery most people are afraid of or run away from. It's almost easier to have tasks than it is to have the job of being you, whatever that looks like.

Our lives continue to expand and grow and change, and every now and again we still check in with each other, asking questions such as: What do you require from me? From our relationship? What can I do to accommodate your needs?

Usually, the request is something so little, a small adjustment that I am happy to make; it never involves cutting off who I am to make him happy. Instead of making things significant, what if you could have a relationship that works and it was easy? What would that look like?

My husband and I keep working and playing together. When something doesn't work, we adjust it, change it, or agree to disagree, but it is never a deal breaker, at least not up to this point. We are willing to discuss it, and that is what is vital to me: the willingness to change when change is required and the willingness to honor both of us, recognizing that a choice for me does not have to be a choice against him.

How does it get any better than that?

This chapter is an excerpt from the upcoming book
Dancing with Riches.

About the Author
Kass Thomas

Kass Thomas is an inspirational speaker, best-selling author, coach, and facilitator at Access Consciousness® for people who are ready to discover their true nature and choose more in their lives. Through her books, workshops, and international in-demand tours, she's here to help you create more ease with communication, your money flows, your business, your relationships, and your body while recognizing the magic you be simply by being you.

Kass is currently touring her new book *7 Steps to Flawless Communication* and facilitating workshops on the 7 simple steps that invite people to change their lives dynamically by communicating more effectively with their bodies, in their relationships, and in their businesses.

And when she's not touring the world teaching people how to live a better life, you can find her entertaining guests at her boutique bed & breakfast in Rome, Italy.

Meet Kass Thomas and get ready to live abundantly. www.KassThomas.com

The Genesis

BY DONNA HALL-HILDEBRAND

What is a Genesis? Some words that are synonymous with genesis are origin, beginning, start, and formation. Some others include development, emergence, creation, evolution, and source! As I've wondered about new beginnings and the creation of my desires with my own marriage, I especially love to reflect on the final synonym of genesis I mentioned: Source.

What does "being the source of your own life and your relationships" mean? For me, I am now choosing to be the source of my life and relationships by acknowledging that I have created everything that shows up in my reality: the good, the bad, and the ugly. The power in acknowledging that I create all of it, even the chaos, allows me to find value in everything I create, and it empowers me to know that I can also change it or use it to my advantage, instead of allowing it to destroy me. By choosing something different,

I will at least change some aspect of it, and therefore I can come to a new beginning, no matter where I've been.

Don't we always seem to enjoy the beginning of our relationships the most? In contrast, the end is called "The End" for a reason, usually a result of some events that we did not enjoy.

What's unique about the beginning that creates so much enjoyment for us? What is it that produces the expansive experience and possibilities of being in discovery, wonder, allowance, gratitude, and play when we begin new relationships?

In the beginning...

In the beginning...there was **ME**! I was 42 years old and creating a new start. My love life had consisted of a series of long-term relationships followed by a 3-year marriage and a second marriage of 13 years. After that marriage dissolved, I was on my own again and more than that, I was choosing me, receiving me, honoring me, and being the source of my life. I was using the tools of consciousness to live my life to the fullest. I was willing to be without judgment of myself and my choices, as well as others and their choices. In this judgment-free space, I was exploring things I had never given myself permission to explore before, like loving my body exactly the way it was; dating just for the fun and discovery of it; being sexual; making choices that made me happy; allowing others to judge me; and being willing to receive everything that showed up in my life—once again: the good, the bad, and the ugly. I knew that I was the creator of my own reality! I was the source of it all, and no matter what showed up. I owned that creation, and I allowed others to own their creations or realities without a point of view about any of it. This was the most freedom I had ever experienced.

After separating from my ex-husband, a friend asked me, "What do you want now? Do you want a relationship again?" And, "If you had a relationship, what would you like it to be like?" I had no idea! I wasn't sure if I wanted another relationship or if I thought I should, as that's what society and this reality told me I should want. If I created a new relationship, I had no idea what I would even like it to look like, because I didn't know what choices there were. I had never started from the space of knowing what I would like. I had never dated before! As soon as one relationship was over, the next person I went out with or kissed became my next relationship; every relationship was long term because I would do whatever I could to stay, even if it wasn't really working. In response to my friend's question, I considered dating as an avenue to explore and taste all the flavors instead of dating as a way to establish a relationship. I would use the dates as a discovery of what I desired in a partner, in a man, and with myself in relationship, but without creating a relationship.

I signed up on a dating site and began meeting men. Before going on a date, I would always ask the questions below. Each question would create awareness. However, if I didn't get a yes to the first three questions, there was no date.

1. Will it be easy?

2. Will it be fun?

3. Body, would you like to play with him and have sex with him? (Asking this question didn't imply

that I would have sex with my date, but why go out with them if my body already knows that it wouldn't enjoy the sex? I would always ask this question again, right before the possibility of sex, just in case my body had received a new awareness since the first time I asked.)

4. Will it be a contribution to my life, my living, and my body?

5. Will it help me create more money in my life?

6. Will it be expansive?

7. Will they be grateful?

Within only a few weeks of dating and asking these questions, I attracted someone who was willing to be in a space similar to me.

Being with this guy was easy and fun. He was dating for the joy of it and for the opportunity to meet new people. He was a "go with the flow" kind of guy who loved receiving what was in the moment and being present to living. I got a "yes" for every single question I asked before going out with him. He was playful, adventurous, and in wonder from moment to moment; savoring, allowing, trusting, creating, and choosing to be so many elements of living that were lighting me up.

As time went on, it felt so light for me to keep moving forward with him. The idea of a relationship still scared me a bit, but each time I felt scared I would ask a question, like "What will my life be like in five years if I choose this relationship?" The awareness I would then receive always created an enthusiasm to continue. What scared me was really my past, and the projections and definitions that came from others about relationships. At the same time, I sensed an ease and delight about creating a relationship with him. We often talked about how our relationship might inspire new possibilities for others in relationships.

After hearing what the founder and co-founder of Access Consciousness® Gary Douglas and Dr. Dain Heer proposed as "The 3 elements to creating the foundation of a good relationship," we felt confident that we were off to the best start either of us had ever created thus far. The three elements are:

1. The person is good in bed

2. They provide money

3. They allow you to do whatever you want to do when you want to do it, and you allow them to do whatever they want to do when they want to do it.

Since we were looking to create a relationship that was easy (by incorporating the three elements above), AND intimate, we also knew that we needed to have "The 5 elements of intimacy for a great relationship: Honor, Trust, Vulnerability, Allowance, and Gratitude," Being all these elements with each other seemed to come naturally to us. This is what I was calling a "conscious relationship."

Crumbling the Conscious Relationship

Within six months, my enjoyable partner sold his home of 16 years that he loved, quit his job of 20 years, and moved over 300 miles to live with me. The first few months were wonderful! Not only did I feel confident that we were creating a conscious relationship, this relationship was greater and more expansive than anything I had ever imagined.

However, within a short amount of time, I started giving up pieces of me and stopped choosing to be conscious. I now know that I stopped choosing the elements of what I knew consciousness was. Instead, I had switched into trying to get it right and trying to keep the fantasy alive. This is not what consciousness is at all. Consciousness is not about getting it right. Getting something right is a judgment. ***Consciousness includes everything and judges nothing.***

Our relationship began to feel too comfortable to me. We were having sex less often, and I felt less connected. When I would try talking with him about my concerns, I would create a sense of him being a disappointment for me. His response was often, "I am sorry I have disappointed you." This would only frustrate me more because I didn't want him to feel like a disappointment. I wanted him to feel invited to be everything I knew him to be. Needless to say, I wasn't exactly being the fun, playful, easy-going, adventurous, sexy girl I had been when we first met. I also wasn't giving him the space to show up as the playful, easy-going, creative, sexy guy he had been either. Instead, I was too busy creating expectations of him, judging how well he was or was not fulfilling my expectations, and projecting onto him how he should be for our relationship to be expansive like it used to be.

Somewhere along the way, I concluded that I had to get this relationship right or I would be "settling." For me, settling meant I was going to accept a status quo relationship and partner instead of an extraordinary relationship and partner. Even though our relationship was still better than any other relationship I had ever created before, I felt like I was compromising because I was comparing it to a fantasy instead of creating each day anew. I had stopped being in discovery of who he was, and started relating to him from my past. Instead of being in allowance, I began living in and creating an exchange program with him as a way to defend against settling. Instead of being the way I would enjoy being with him, I did what I thought I should in order to get him to respond as I expected. Somewhere, I stopped being the source of my life and began making him and our relationship responsible for how my life could or could not be. I abandoned being in question and shifted my focus onto the very thing I was trying to protect myself from creating: a relationship which required me to "settle." I was unwilling to see that the only thing I was settling on was my own unwillingness to be the creator and the source of my own reality and my relationship.

Never Too Late to Begin Again

Once I saw the trap I had created for myself, I began looking at the conclusions and judgments I had created and chose to ask some questions instead. With each question I asked, I gained a greater awareness of how I had created everything!

I asked, "Are you willing to be, for yourself, everything you think he should be for you?"

I had concluded that my lover didn't desire me as much as he used to, so I asked myself, "Are you willing to desire and adore yourself as much as you wish he would desire and adore you?" By asking this question, I began to see that I wasn't feeling any desire for myself. Instead, I was feeling entitlement! How desirable and inviting do you think that was? Not so much!

I also asked myself, "Are you willing to create your own life in a way that lights you up?" I realized that if I was lit up about my own life, I was more likely to light up our relationship.

Next, I asked, "Are you willing to be the conscious one in the relationship by choosing to change and receive?" Then I acknowledged that it's not about getting it right or being in competition with each other regarding who is doing more for the relationship.

Finally, I asked, "Are you willing to be everything that you ask of your relationship, like being sexy, fun, adventurous, playful, and engaging? Are you willing to be everything for yourself and receive yourself totally and in every moment?" These questions gave me the awareness that all the judgments, expectations, and projections I had been creating, destroyed my capacity to receive myself or him in our relationship.

Focusing on what I didn't want instead of asking questions to create what I desired, limited my ability to be a conscious partner. I was not creating what I desired with him, our relationship, sex, or myself. I cut off receiving from him the moment I started judging him, and I was unaware that I was creating competition and had stopped gifting. After reading the following by Gary Douglas in *Money Isn't The Problem, You Are*, I remembered what was unique about the way I was being in my relationship in the beginning, and I tapped back into my capacities with receiving, gifting, choosing, and creating a conscious relationship again.

"With gifting, there is no separate exchange that occurs. You give without expectation of return, and as a result, you simultaneously receive without limit. The gifting is the receiving, and the receiving is the gifting, all at the same time. With gifting and receiving, you have the elements that allow you to truly have a sense of communion with all things. When you go out in nature, for example, does it gift to you? Does it expect anything in return? Nature gifts everything it has at all times, and it simultaneously receives from everything. The fruit trees create the fruit and gift to you totally. Do they hold any of it back? When you have a flowerbed full of beautiful flowers, they gift to you their fragrance and their beauty, and they ask nothing in return. What they receive from you is the energy you give them and the gratitude you have for their beauty."

New Worlds Are Created...

I have discovered again, that one of the ways I can receive and gift the most is by being all the energies of sexualness. **Sexualness** *is the nurturing, healing, caring, creative, joyful, orgasmic, expansive energy of life itself.* When I became aware that I had cut off much of my sexualness shortly after my partner moved in, I began choosing again to embody those energies, first with myself and then with him, from a much greater space of vulnerability. As I did so, I started choosing beyond my expectations, projections, judgments, and conclusions about what he might think, what he might want, how he might respond, and even how he may or may not (mostly how he may not) reciprocate. For example, I made a point every week to nurture his body with sensual massage, taking the time to light candles in the room, play sexy music, and heat damp towels in the crock pot to add the element of yummy warm towels on his feet, hands, face, chest, neck, back, and genitals at different times during the massage. I really went all–out. I didn't choose this with the expectation of nurturing in return, but from the willingness to be and receive the sexual energy my body was being as I gifted this to his body. I had also become more vocal about what I'd love to receive from him (again, from the space of invitation without expectation... knowing I can be all that for myself, if I choose). In addition to all I was being and receiving for myself, I was asking the question, "What will it take for him to nurture my body in a delicious way?" knowing that I would be able to receive that too, if and when it showed up.

After three weeks of being this for myself and with him, I came home one evening, and he asked if we could relax and have a glass of wine. I went and put on my new, upgraded robe and poured us each a glass. As I sat on the couch, he played some music for me on his turntable. (He collects and listens to music on vinyl, and we refer to it as his "vinyl fetish.") He played "Ain't No Woman Like The One I Got" by The Four Tops... and he danced for me!!!! He had me giggling with pure joy and delight, adoring him! I had previously sent him a YouTube video I saw on Facebook of a guy dancing in a fun, sexy, playful way, and I playfully mentioned to him that I would love it if he would dance like this for me. After the music was over, he took off my robe, and he tucked my body into a delicious fluffy soft blanket.... Then he started kissing and rubbing my feet, continuing to move up my body until he had kissed, massaged, and caressed every part of me.

WOW!!! He nurtured my body with such kind, generous, connected, sensual and sexual energy. I absolutely loved the playfulness with the song and the dancing! It tickled my soul, making me smile in the most wonderful way! Somehow I was completely relaxed, even though I had a gigantic smile on my face most of the time, while he was massaging me, caressing me, tickling my body with his curly thick head of hair, kissing me, licking me, and playfully keeping me covered (except where he was nurturing my body). Mmmmm Mmmmm Mmmmm!!! It literally knocked me out, like a smiling baby in dreamland!

The New Genesis of a Conscious Relationship

As I am choosing me, receiving me, honoring me, and being everything for me, every day has the possibility of being totally new. Our relationship gets to surprise me and feel new each day as I reflect on the gratitude I feel from choosing consciousness. I am the source of my life and my relationship, and with that reality, our relationship is better than ever. When something shows up that isn't a match with what I desire to create, I now ask, "How can I receive more of me in this moment? How can I receive more of me in this relationship?"

What if we could see every moment in our relationships as a new opportunity to receive and create a genesis of new possibilities? What if this moment is where new desires originate and it's never too late to begin again, start anew, emerge into a new space, and create a new energy? Isn't that what evolving is all about, progressing and expanding from where you are?

About the Author
Donna Hall-Hildebrand

Donna Hall-Hildebrand is a life and energy coach, an intuitive healer, advanced massage therapist, and a facilitator of transformation. With over 20 years in the wellness industry, Donna has enjoyed helping individuals reconnect to their own knowing, talents, abilities, and capabilities to restore both vitality in their body and potency in their being. She has a great desire to show others a new reality with their bodies, where kindness and gratitude are present and judgment of bodies is removed.

Donna is a Certified Access Consciousness® Bars Facilitator and Practitioner, Certified Practitioner of The Balance Your Life® Energy Coaching Program, and a Certified One Command® Practitioner. She has participated in A Course in Awareness®, Landmark Education® Curriculum for Living "Coaching" and "Leadership" Programs, and studied many other transformational methods and energy modalities. These have all contributed greatly to her understanding of how to use energy and provided the many tools that she shares with others for greater ease in getting out of judgment, removing barriers, clearing limitations, creating possibilities, and living a life of choice.

The acceptance Donna has for people gives them an opportunity to be in allowance with where they are at any moment. Donna's willingness to look at herself and openly share with a sense of "realness" generates a refreshing experience for those she works with. Combining that with her genuine enthusiasm, she leaves people motivated and empowered to act. She creates a level of comfort and clarity that allows people to come to awareness quickly.

Donna is always questioning how life can be FUN, EASY, and JOYFUL! What if there is a master switch that enables you to create anything, and that master switch is you? What if you can create everything you desire from the outside, simply by awakening the energy that is already within you by creating a life and body that turns you on?

You can visit Donna's independent website to find out more about her bodywork, private coaching sessions, group coaching and programs at: www.innergeticawakenings.com

From Martyr Wife to Happy Life

By Sadie Lake

Have you ever noticed that when you're trying to make changes in your life, whether you want to eat healthier, work out more, save money or pay off debt, the harder you try and the more effort you use, the farther away your goal seems to get? Like when you go on a diet and start working out, and somehow manage to gain more weight than you lose? Or have you experienced the "rubber band effect" where you set a goal and make giant leaps forward when you start, but later rebound to a place farther back than you were when you began? Have you wondered why that might be?

I have selected the words to describe these scenarios very deliberately; words like *trying* and *goals*. Words are energy, and when it comes to our physical realities, energy is the basic building block creating what eventually becomes matter and circumstance. What do you notice when you sense the difference between the energies of the words *try* and *choose*. When we say we'll *try* to do something, the likelihood of us actually doing it can range anywhere from 0% to 100% depending on how much we value the result. *Choice*, on the other hand, is an unequivocal YES; we're doing it, no matter what. When we set a *goal,* we basically come to a solidified conclusion about what we've decided is a better or more correct thing to have or be, and in so doing, tend to judge ourselves relentlessly for everywhere we aren't already at our goal. And because "what we resist, persists" we often end up creating more of what we don't desire than what we do. How often in our relationships, whether it be with our partner, children, parents, friends, or colleagues, do we set a goal of trying to be more or less a certain way—more patient, more generous, or less critical? Has it ever worked for longer than two seconds?

One of the interesting things I've become aware of is that relationships are like a game of chess; not against another person, though, as it may seem, but against oneself. We sit on our high-horse, calculating our words and actions. We want to be "the bigger person," but often when it comes to choosing something that would create a greater situation for the whole, that sub-conscious, ego-centric "self" sitting on the other side of the table moves in opposition. This often shows up between partners when one person decides the other isn't supporting them enough. So in retaliation, they become reluctant to give the other partner what they require and desire in return.

In the early years of my marriage, I played this game a lot. I always ended up stuck in a checkmate of my opposing points of view. I subconsciously believed that a stay-at-home mom wasn't as valuable a contribution to the family or to society as a "breadwinner." Nonetheless, staying home with my kids was damn hard work! It was self-created work; but hard nonetheless. I was constantly defending how difficult it was, pointing out how I never got a moment to do what *I* wanted to do. I didn't "get to" shower or go to the bathroom alone. Wah, wah, wah. My husband just didn't understand what it was like being poor little me. So I took it upon myself to educate him about the sorrow and difficulty of my situation. I was so focused on *my* world I couldn't (or wouldn't) be sympathetic about what was going on in his. I wouldn't allow myself to acknowledge that he had struggles of his own with the pressure of providing all of our financial resources as well as our physical and emotional security. From this place of feeling undervalued and unappreciated, neither of us were willing to let go of defending ourselves and choose a different possibility—one that could potentially change all this.

Let's be clear here.... It's not that we didn't see, with total clarity, that our stubbornness was creating the total opposite of what we both desired for our relationship. I kept being a martyr, illogically buying the idea that my martyrdom would somehow make my husband exalt me as the greatest, most perfect, self-sacrificing Mother Theresa-esque wife and mother who ever lived. I was energetically pulling so hard for his validation that, to him, it probably felt like his universe would collapse if he gave it to me. He had withdrawn and gone numb, knowing that I was never going to sing his praises when the only words to escape my lips were litanies of complaints. We had many, many conversations about what we both desired and required:

to feel appreciated, valued, and understood. We also both knew that if we could just muster the strength to give what the other seemed so desperately to need, each of our metaphorical buckets would be filled. Instead, we each kept choosing the immediate gratification of the "Kingdom of Me," rather than that which would create greater for the whole, the "Kingdom of We."

While this may seem like a battle between partners, in truth, it is one's own opposing points of view that create the dichotomy. My point of view (that my role as a mother was not valuable) was juxtaposed with my direct experience (spending all day selflessly focused on the needs of my children and knowing how valuable I was to them). My belief that my husband didn't know what it was like to "do my job" conflicted with the truth that I was too much of a martyr ever to let him do any part of my job.

Each time we stick ourselves with a point of view by coming to a conclusion, it's like moving a pawn in our own game; the bigger the conclusion, the more powerful the player. My Rook, the sneaky little prankster that ultimately locked me in checkmate, was the underlying point of view that I seemed to be clinging to for dear life like a buoy of unconsciousness keeping me barely afloat in my cesspool of misery: the belief that I hadn't wanted kids in the first place. Whether or not this was still my point of view was irrelevant. I had *decided* it was true and was, therefore, defending it to the death—more accurately, to my own slow, torturous locked-in-a-house-with-no-one-to-talk-to-but-a-baby death. With this metaphorical hole in my bucket, no amount of praise could have filled it. Until I was willing to let go of defending why I was unhappy—

because I was holding on so tight to the idea that what I had created wasn't actually what I wanted—I couldn't look pragmatically at what else I could choose. That's why I say that relationships are like a game of chess...against oneself. In many ways, it doesn't actually matter what your partner is or isn't doing if you're not willing to look, with total vulnerability, at what your reality is and what your own points of view are creating.

What if everything is the opposite of what it appears to be, and nothing is the opposite of what it appears to be? Sound crazy? That's why in Access Consciousness® we call this "the crazy phrase." Do you remember playing with convex lenses in science class as a kid? Convex lenses are pieces of curved class like the contact lenses people wear in their eyes. I see the energy of "the crazy phrase" like a convex lens: when you're looking at it from your own personal, zoomed in Kingdom of Me point of view, what you're looking at appears normal and correct to you. But when you back up and look at the big picture, or the zoomed out Kingdom of We viewpoint, the image actually inverts, now appearing upside down. Applying this example to relationships, when we look through the lens of our own point of view, things look right and correct. But, when we zoom out and include everyone in the computation of the equation, we often see that everything is indeed the opposite of what it appeared to be. The Kingdom of Me is often the literal inverse of the Kingdom of We. Everything is the opposite of what it appears to be.

I see this principle play out in relationships all the time. When we're trying to choose something that creates greater for everyone, we often leave ourselves out of the equation, thereby creating less for ourselves instead of being included in the "greater" that we're creating for others. Take, for example, mothers (parents) who decide they need to give up their lives for their children. Their lives can become so small and contracted that they're left withering away, cut off from the joy, hobbies, and interests that previously supplied such robust energy to their lives.

In partnerships, this shows up when we choose what seems gratifying in the moment, but we don't look at what that choice is creating for our future—for everyone's future. You've likely seen this happen when one partner gives up doing the things they love in order to spend more time with the other or to try to make them happy. Picture the traditional scenario where guys give up going out for beers with their buddies to sit at home and watch movies with their girlfriends; or when women stop being independent and fun and instead become codependent and naggy. Initially, it appears that our choice will create what we want: whatever gratification we're getting from being with our partner. But in the end, it creates the opposite: woman replaces her friends with her man, who is not interested in hearing about every detail of her life, and therefore starts to tune her out.

Let me ask you this: In your long term relationships, what was it that drew you to that person in the first place? Were those traits or characteristics still present at the relationship's end? If you fell in love with your man because of his fun joviality and sense of humor, is that what you get from him when he sits at home listening to you drone on about why the lady in the cubicle next to you is driving you nuts? If your girlfriend used to be assertive and confident, did that assertive, sexy edge change from flirty banter into critical nagging when you didn't execute all her unspoken expectations?

Let's all be honest, whether we want to admit it or not, women tend to default to nagging to get what they want, and men tend to resort to "tuning out" to avoid being nagged and made wrong. As a kid, I watched this scenario play out over and over between my parents. My mom had the expectation that because my step-dad was the man, he should take out the garbage (whose point of view was that anyway?!). When he didn't do it, she'd either nag him in a condescending tone, or do it herself in her best passive-aggressive, melodramatic style to mime how annoyed she was; because of course, she couldn't just come right out in her normal tone of voice and ask, "Hey lover, would you mind taking out the garbage?" This is just one example, but the general theme was omnipresent in their interactions. Mom's message: You're wrong. You're too stupid to pick up on the telepathic expectations I sent you, and since you didn't do what I expected you to do, you're a bad person. Step Dad message: La La La...I'm sorry, were you talking to me? I couldn't hear you because I've become deaf to the tones of condescension.

Sound familiar?

You see, somehow in the moment we think that acting out our frustrations with nagging and complaining, or tuning out and ignoring, will work out well for us. It never does. It never creates something greater to disregard or belittle our partner, our children, or anyone else.

So what does work? What does it look like to choose the Kingdom of We?

Choosing for the Kingdom of We starts with a simple question: "What is *my* point of view here? What have I bought as true, that maybe isn't?" When we become aware of our points of view, we can look at them without walls or defenses and ask, "Ok, what is this point of view *creating* in my life?" To this day, my husband will only vacuum the floor if I'm not home. Early in our marriage, I seared him with my hot poker of superior-bitchdom by getting out the vacuum after he had just finished and going over his work because I didn't think he had done a good enough job the first time. He is still scarred from that experience. At the time, I'm sure I thought that he would say, "Oh! THAT'S how you do it! Silly me! I'll be sure to spend three hours vacuuming next time so that it's perfect. Forgive me; I'll never do it wrong again." He didn't. Instead, he did what any self-respecting man would (and often does) do: he decided he would never vacuum again. If I wanted it perfect, I could do it myself.

Choosing for the Kingdom of We is looking at the big picture: "If I do this, what does that create?" You have to be willing to see WHAT IS, not what you hope will be, based on some utopian ideal. If I nag, what does that create for my lover? If I tune my woman out every time she talks, what is that going to create? If she feels like I never listen to her and that I don't value what's important to her, will I get more blow jobs or fewer? It's that simple folks! What if everything is the opposite of what it appears to be and nothing is the opposite of what it appears to be?

This often brings up interesting points of view…"So, if I choose for the Kingdom of We instead of the Kingdom of Me, is my partner going to reciprocate? Or will s/he take advantage of my generosity? Is it going to be all give and never get?" These are great questions! Maybe yes, maybe no. What came first, the chicken or the egg? Who cares! Do you like the push/pull you have going on now? What if this could actually be the litmus test for whether or not this particular person is someone you want to have as a partner? Is it important to you to be with someone who has your back? Does your partner have your back now?

To find out, you may start with your "deal and deliver" conversation: "Hey, what is it that you desire of me? What would you like our relationship to be like?" After you both get clear on what it is that you and your partner both require and desire, (because who are we kidding, how is your partner supposed to deliver what you desire if you never tell them what that is?) the first step is to look critically at whether you actually can or even want to be what the other is looking for. If so, then you make the choice to be and do whatever it is that they require as it creates greater for the Kingdom of We, unequivocally. Notice I didn't say *try*? This is a choice. The "bigger you" is calling the shots here. You're not getting checkmated by that "little you" on the other side of the game board. You're *choosing* to give them what they're asking for, and to have their back in a way maybe no one ever has. The reason I put such emphasis on this being a CHOICE is that if you *try* to do this from a place of obligation, it will not work out well. When we *try*, rather than *choose*, on some level we are doing it because we have a judgment that we "should." When we decide something *should* be so, it is no longer a choice, but an obligation. I don't know about you, but when I perceive something as an obligation, I end up feeling pissed off and resentful. That is not the energy of *honoring your partner and having their back,* and they will feel it. But you can *choose* to be supportive, and when you notice that sneaky "little you" trying to slip its judgments into the back of your mind—*he didn't pick up his socks off the bathroom floor... he never listens*—you say, "NO. I'm not going there," and send her back to her side of the table.

How do you keep Little You in check? CHOOSE GRATITUDE. This is the secret. You've heard it before, and it seems so simple, but here's why it works: gratitude and judgment cannot coexist. Want to keep that Kingdom of Me "you" in her place? Look for and express gratitude for your partner. Start showing them how grateful you are for them just being them, and for the little things they do. How do you know how to do that? First, remember and follow through with what they told you in your "deal and deliver" conversation. And second, give them sex. Ladies, this is how you show a man how grateful you are for him. Men, this may or may not work for you...you may have to do the unspeakable: TALK to your woman. I know, it's like pulling your nose hairs out one at a time, but it will get you more of what you want; it will get you more sex. Have you ever noticed that women need to feel connected to deliver sex and that men require sex to feel connected? Another example of how everything is the opposite of what it appears to be and nothing is the opposite of what it appears to be?!

This all reminds me of something I learned in one of my college Psychology classes.... Researchers performed an experiment on vision in which they gave subjects eye glasses that inverted (turned upside down) everything they saw. Interestingly, after just a short time, their brains reverted the image, allowing them to see normally through the glasses, instead of upside down. This makes me wonder...in our relationships, if we would be willing to suffer the temporary disorientation and discomfort of looking at our choices from the Kingdom of We, could we just as easily adjust to that as our new normal? What if everything is the opposite of what it appears to be and nothing is the opposite of what it appears to be?

About the Author
Sadie Lake

Sadie Lake knows that something else is possible for all of us here on Planet Earth. Her greatest joy is in being is a facilitator, educator, and catalyst for the creation of a new reality—one that primarily functions from question, choice, possibility, and consciousness.

Her first book, *Creations: Conscious Fertility and Conception, Pregnancy and Birth* aims to create change in the place it all begins: conception through birth. The sequel, *Possibilities in Parenting*, tackles the next frontier for creating a different possibility: the foundational relationship between parent and child.

Sadie lives in Spokane, WA, where she gets to practice what she teaches every day as a wife and mother to three infinite beings... in little girls' bodies.

When she's not cooking, cleaning, or feeding said infinite beings, she travels the world teaching classes and working one-on-one with people just like you who are interested in choosing something greater. Find her on Facebook as Sadie Lake ~Facilitator, Educator, Catalyst~

A New Reality in Relationships

BY YURYRA GUZMAN

Have you ever wondered what more is really possible in relationships? How after being "in love," it seems to be easy to be "in hate" with the same person? Why is it so complicated to be happy in a relationship?

Are we missing something? What percentage of the people in relationships you know have the kind of relationship you would desire?

Many times during my life, I found myself crying in the middle of the night feeling lonely. I feared that to be alone was a confirmation that I was not a good person. When I was with someone, I gave up many parts of me to stay with them even if they weren't even kind to me. I felt so angry about men! And pretty confused as well.

What if we could create a world where people we cared for were kind to one another? Why don't I see a relationship that I would love to have? Is it possible to have a relationship in which everybody is happy? Those were my questions for many years. I still have questions, but now they are a little different.

My Fairy Tale...Well, not really

I was a shy teenager, shyer in the field of boys. I grew up feeling separated from men—they were from a planet far away—a cool, distant, mean one. I learned, *Be smart. If I'm not, they will hurt me and break my heart!* There was a mischievous, charming side of them that enchanted me. With all my mixed up points of view and the significance I put on men, I went unsurprisingly from emotionally abusive relationships to ones that I call "no count" with people who were nice to me—but whom I did not feel really attracted to, then to others so I wouldn't be alone, and on to "Will you love me someday as I love you?"

Aren't you loving my telenovela? "Your point of view creates your reality," as my friend Dr. Dain Heer likes to say. I was cast perfectly in my drama of love and no love. I was the queen and the victim, the one who would shine when true love, soulmate, "meant to be together forever" showed up, then losing myself every time I desperately looked for someone who could love me, repeating the same story over and over.

There were nice guys who wanted to be with me and because they did I found them less likable. Who in his sane mind would choose me? Oh, did I mention yet that I had a very poor concept of myself? On the other hand, I had the attractive guys who were not exactly kind to me, but somehow I always thought that one day the power of my love would change them, make them adore me, and treat me like the rightful princess I was. Oh, the joy!

One day (was it really one day?) I gave it all up. I couldn't sustain the illusion. I concluded that I was not the right material for relationships. There was not a right man for me; I would get old and die alone! Instead, I decided I would enjoy the fact there was not a person for me in this life—I would live life my way. I created a different life: friends, parties, joyful trips, a successful executive career, and fun dating. After a while, I realized I still was missing something. It was not that I felt alone; it was a lack of choice that was disturbing my "perfect single life."

I was not single by choice. I was single because of my conclusion and judgment that no man was worth it and love was not for me. I was creating my life from resistance. It took me years to get around my judgments about men, myself, and relationships, and to choose to create a relationship. Today I am married and creating a relationship that works for us in communion, allowance, and continuous gratitude, moment by moment.

If you are in a situation like I was, I would like to shorten your process with what I've learned, if you choose it.

Someday my prince will come, but in the meantime…

What if the best way to wait for Mr. Right or Ms. "The One" is by living your life fully? If we wait to live until the person of our dreams shows up, we are making the relationship so significant that it throws our life out of balance. When your relationship is something that you can add to your life rather than being a substitute for it, you take the significance off the relationship and your partner. It opens the possibility for both to have a life after love.

Some interesting points of view about relationships

If I have to tell him, he doesn't love me. Did you buy the idea that love gives the other person the capacity to read your mind? *If he really, truly loves me, he will know how to please me!* Have you decided that love gives the special capacity to know what the other person desires, requires, and how they like things done? If you require something, SAY IT! Ask clearly, without asking the other person to read between the lines. Never assume your loved one knows something that you never ask for.

I don't need anybody! This is true, but if we reject everyone and separate ourselves because we don't "need anybody," it is like moving into a hole, separated from everything and everybody. What if being with someone else is a choice, not a need? Women, would you be willing to receive everything a man is willing to give you? Most men were raised to show their love by doing. They love to do stuff for women! Everybody wants to be received, and receiving gracefully is an invitation to gift more. Yet it is something most of us aren't very good at. For some of us receiving implies compromise, obligation, and expectations.

Men are from a different planet! Are they from a DIFFERENT planet like Mars or Saturn, or are we just different? What if the differences between the sexes didn't mean either sex was wrong? Would it be possible to embrace

those differences and use them to our advantage—each of us using our strengths to create something greater?

I can fix him/her! Many times I have heard things like "He has potential, I just have to change/train/educate him." Where is the kindness here? What if, instead of choosing a person who you think needs to be fixed to be how you want him to be, you chose somebody who you already like the way he is? Many times women do things to try to change a man with the implication that men are stupid, incompetent, unreliable, or good for nothing, and they need to be fixed to become acceptable. A workable relationship is actually seeing the person you are with, not expecting them to be something they are not.

Women: Don't share your feelings! I can imagine you saying, "What? What do you mean I should not share my feelings; relationships are all about that!" Are they? Women cannot believe men don't care about their feelings because feelings are what run most women's lives. How much time and effort have you invested in an attempt to get men to listen to your feelings? How has that worked for you? When you ask your man to listen to your feelings you are asking him to be something he is not. If you want to share your feelings, get a girlfriend; if you want to have a lover don't make him your girlfriend. What if we don't make that wrong?

There are hundreds of points of view that bring frustration, anger and broken hearts instead of ease and joy in relationships. If they haven't worked, would you consider letting them go? You can say every day, "All of the judgments I have about relationships and the other sex, I destroy and uncreate them all." Each day you can also destroy everything your relationship was; this would give you a new start every day, but you don't want to have that much ease and possibility, do you?

A Divorceless Relationship

Divorce is a strong word for many of us. I used to fear it because I defined divorce as failure. I avoided relationships so I would not be in danger of ever getting a divorce. Now I know that the divorce I was always afraid of was the divorce from myself. Please, don't ever give up yourself, never any part or fragment of you. Be you in totality, no matter what. How many times have you cut out any part of yourself to have or keep a relationship? Have you left behind who you are in order to be who you (or others) decided you should be? Are you designing your relationships to please somebody else?

The definition of relationship is the distance or separation between two objects. If you are in a relationship with me, that means you are not with me. Relationship creates separation and takes away the possibility of oneness. People go into relationship and then begin divorcing parts of themselves to make the relationship "work." They start changing themselves, divorcing pieces of who they are and pretty soon they don't show up fully. Eventually, they have divorced so much of who they had been in the beginning that they have nothing in common anymore.

Do you have a secret agenda in your relationship? Are you using relationship to prove or validate your worth or value? Does relationship mean a specific social or financial status? For some people, relationships define them as winner or loser. A secret agenda is something that is lying beneath your awareness, secret even to you, and it gives the energy to choose things for crazy reasons.

A relationship in 10 second increments. We like to have things settled, known and decided. The problem is that doesn't leave us much ability to adjust to what is actually happening in reality. Instead, if we choose every 10 seconds, the pressure to make the "right choice" vanishes. When any choice you make is only good for 10 seconds, you make a choice for your relationship and see what that choice creates. If you like the result, you can make the same choice for the next 10 seconds. If you don't, you can make another choice! Living in 10 second increments gives you the space to live in the present, not in the past or for the future.

What if, instead of being interested in relationship, you were interested in communion? Communion is an energetic communication. Having communion with yourself, you can have communion with others. When you are in communion, you are energetically connected with anyone and everything. If you are looking for real communion and not more separation you must be conscious.

Creating a relationship that works for You

Are you creating relationships thinking of what works for everybody but you? Is your target in relationships to make others happy? Would you consider the possibility of including yourself in a relationship? Everything about relationship is learned—often learned badly. We have been educated mostly by people with dysfunctional relationships in which they disappear into the partnership and don't exist as individuals anymore. When I got married and said, "Yes, I do," I meant, "Yes I'll be myself, and be the space for you where you can be you, and be in love with life and our life together. Yes, I desire to co-create with you something greater than I could create by myself."

But then, how do I keep my vows? How do we create a relationship that works? What do we do to keep our love alive? I had seen so many instances in which love was not enough to keep two people together that I was a little confused about love as the main ingredient for a long, happy marriage. What does love mean anyway? The meaning of the word love is different for every person; it includes a beautiful package of conclusions, expectations, and judgments. That is one of the reasons we get confused when we "love" someone.

What does love mean to you? Are you aware of what you mean when you say, "I love you"? Being honest, I never was! And I never asked the other person what he meant by "love." What if there are pragmatic elements for a good relationship that are easier to understand than "love"? The components for a good relationship are the elements of great intimacy.

Allowance - Allowance is looking at everything as an interesting point of view. It is allowing another's point of view to be just their point of view, without a need to resist and react to it or align and agree with it, without a desire to change it, or even have any opinion or significance about it. Allowance takes you out of the place where you believe you know better than someone else about what he or she should be doing or being. Does that sound like a hard to place to be? How would it be to have total allowance for yourself, for your choices, and for the other person's choices? In my personal point of view, it is hard to have the other elements of intimacy if you don't first have allowance.

Vulnerability - Unfortunately there is the misconception that to be vulnerable means to be weak, undefended, and an easy target to be hurt. In actuality, vulnerability is the capacity that allows you to receive. You build up walls to protect you, and then hide behind those walls, which creates separation between the Universe and you, and it becomes almost impossible to receive anything through your walls. True vulnerability is the greatest protection ever; it keeps you from being hurt, not by defending, but by being aware—when you are willing to receive, perceive, to know and be everything. It requires you to lower all your barriers and be willing to reveal yourself to others so they can see who you truly are. And the bonus is that when you have no barriers, you get to perceive who and what they are as well.

Honor - Honor means to always treat the other person with regard, respect, admiration, and affection. Rudeness, unkindness, and cruelty honor no one. Honor is an element that will allow you to flow gracefully even when you are crazy mad at your significant other.

Trust - Trust is to know that the person will do what they will do—not what you hope, desire, believe, dream, or wish they would do. The truth is that people do what they choose to do until they choose something else. Trust is not about blind faith. It is not to see what you want, but what already is. If you function from blind faith, you expect the other person to do what you want them to do, not what they will do, believing that it will turn out as you want it just because you want it.

Gratitude – Gratitude is when you are grateful for someone or something. You are grateful for someone exactly the way they are, not as you demand, expect, or wish them to be—which would be a judgment. Gratitude and judgment are mutually exclusive. When you are in gratitude for another, you expand your reality and theirs.

When you choose real intimacy, you are creating from a more conscious place in which nothing is demanded or required, except the joy of being there in the moment. Then you are creating your relationship. You are not "having a relationship."

Are you interested in creating an intimate relationship with yourself? You can use these five elements. Is it possible to have an intimate relationship with anyone else if you don't have one with yourself?

Conscious Relationships

How can we create a relationship beyond the romantic movie lines "I love him and he loves me"? Is consciousness the key to stopping the insanity we see every day in the way we handle relationships? How would a conscious relationship look? If you are interested in creating a conscious relationship, you will be the conscious person in that relationship, and I have some suggestions for you!

Choose somebody who is going to expand your life and create with you; someone who is an addition to your life, not a substitute for it; somebody who is fun to live with and easy to get along with; somebody with whom you can create something greater than what you could create by yourself.

In a conscious relationship, both people are independent—they keep who they are, what they like, and what they don't like—without divorcing any part of themselves. They choose what works, and don't have to wait for the other to choose for them. They empower each other to be the greatness they truly are, cherishing them to do what makes them happy. They focus on what is required instead of stopping each other, and give the space to each other to be, create, do, and have everything they desire in life.

Conscious partners don't make the other person their life or expect to become the other person's life. They invite their lover to be part of their life and to choose what they'd like to be a part of.

A conscious relationship stays in the question, not in conclusions or expectations: What can I create with this person? How can we out-create our relationship today? What is possible in this relationship that we have not even imagined before?

There are so many possibilities in relationships. I invite you to keep exploring what else really is possible for you. What would it take to reveal all the lies, mysteries, and fantasies about relationships and love? What if it is possible to out-create any relationship we have known until now and institute a reality where we all live in oneness without any separation from us or anyone else?

What is inconceivable today in relationships that could be a new reality in the future?

I wonder... what will you choose?

I look forward to playing with you!!!

About the Author
Yuryra Guzman

Yuryra Guzman is an international Coach of Possibilities. She received her BS from Universidad Autónoma de Guadalajara and her MD in Business from TecMilenio University in Mexico. She brings her experience from a 15-year career in the Human Development and Business field to her work as Playground Hostess, inviting you to play with the energies of your "self," your relationships and this reality with a mix of joyful, seductive and pragmatic tools.

Yuryra is an embodiment enamored, Inconceivable Relationships Wiz, Reiki Master, Body Talk Practitioner, Access Consciousness® and Right Relationship For You™ Certified Facilitator; #1 International Bestselling Author of *Colors of Now* and *I'm Having It*, which was featured on *Ask BonBon* TV Show in New York City.

Yuryra is also a co-host of the Radio Show *Seducing Beyond Limitations* on A2ZEN.FM where she and co-host Rachel Silber explore the energy of seduction as the invitation to create a life with ease, elegance and joy beyond any limitation.

Her enthusiasm for exploring infinite possibilities of joy and play in life coupled with her personal journey and intuitive capacities provided Yuryra with the ability to see directly into another's life and identify the self–defeating, limiting behaviors brought about by conflicting beliefs and patterns learned in life. She has the ability to facilitate others to connect with their seducer within, inviting them to a different way to be in the world and alleviating conditions such as anxiety, poor self-image, and unhealthy/not working relationships.

Yuryra sees a different reality and possibility—usually far beyond this reality which she has used to create her own life. She loves shaking up the supposed hard-set realities and paradigms kept in place over lifetimes to create something greater.

Her knowledge, experience, intuition, total allowance, unique personality, and sense of humor make her a delicious experience of joy and awareness. Yuryra's target is to be a catalyst for a new and inconceivable reality in all kinds of relationships—with our body, our money, others and ourselves.

She has gotten around many limitations she had bought as hers from different sources including culture, family, and society, and is creating a life that finally works for her where she can choose to show up every moment—as be a wife, lover, business entrepreneur, daughter, world traveler, consciousness junkie, and writer—with ease, joy and glory.

Yuryra lives with her husband in Bozeman, Montana, USA where you can find her working in the garden, cooking spicy food, hiking, and trying very hard not to be the worst cross country skier or camper in the Rockies.

Connect with Yuryra at yuryraguzman@gmail.com or find her on Twitter, Instagram or Facebook at Yuryra Guzman-InJoy Playing. Yuryra is available for private one-on-one sessions, personalized individual packages, as well as Skype sessions to serve clients around the world. She also offers teleseminars and workshops worldwide facilitating and empowering others to create a different reality in every area of their life. Find more about the infinite possibilities with Yuryra at www.yuryraguzman.com and www.yuryraguzman.accessconsciousness.com.

Committing to Your Life:

CONSCIOUS COUPLING AND UNCOUPLING

BY JULIE TUTON

What would it be like to enjoy being with your partner, finding new ways to have fun with them and with all the people in your life, that you haven't considered before? And what would it be like to have the freedom to be yourself, and commit to yourself totally? Have you cut off any part of yourself to make things work for your partner? In a contributory relationship, you do not give up your life in favor of theirs. They add to your life and you add to theirs.

This is what I see as possible in a conscious relationship: Consciousness is the awareness of everything without judgment, so in a conscious relationship, there would be no judgment of yourself or the other person. You would be aware of their choices, and whether you agreed or not, you would allow them to choose what they desire (as you choose for you). It creates a greater future when you each choose the things that bring a sense of excitement, possibilities, and joy. And if being together didn't work out, there would be no judgment in moving on.

So, how do you get there?

The difficulty begins with a lack of awareness of self. In the past, I never really thought of myself in regard to the relationship; I only thought of the other person. I was always aware of everything the other person wanted but had no idea what I wanted. And I had a relationship most of my life, starting when I was 12 years old!

Imagine being 12 years old, entering into a relationship and never having an awareness of yourself. I don't know if you've experienced anything like that, but I gave myself up at the drop of a hat. I tried to do whatever it took to make it work for the other person because that's what I could perceive.

Everywhere you have been looking to your partner, or looking outward, rather than including yourself in the computation of your relationship, will you consider changing that perspective?

If you're always looking at what everybody else needs, wants, or desires or what would work for them, you have left yourself out. I recognized that's what I was doing, so I set out 14 years ago to start getting a sense of me. In the search, I found Access Consciousness® and started using the tools to change lots of things in my life that weren't working as well as I would like—business, parenting, sex and relationship, to name a few.

How do you find your point of view? Even though I didn't consider what I wanted and didn't think I knew what I wanted, somewhere deep, deep down inside I knew what I didn't want. At the beginning of each relationship that ended up not working, there was a *whisper of knowing* that I was going against some awareness. Sometimes it felt like a twisted, contracted feeling in my stomach.

You hear people talking about a gut feeling and to follow your gut. But I realized the opposite is true! When you get a twisted, contracted, sinking feeling, you are going against something in you that knows what you are considering is not a good idea. It won't end well. What actually creates a greater future is when you choose the things that give you a sense of excitement, possibilities, expansion, lightness, and joy. This was one of the first things I learned from Access Consciousness. It gave me so much more ease in navigating the choices in life to create more of what I wanted.

It wasn't much of a surprise that after being married for 20 years with two young children, things started to bubble up. Even though we were the "best couple" amongst our friends, I knew underneath the facade I wasn't really happy. During the last five years of that relationship, I applied the Access tools. I thought using the tools would fix my relationship. Further, I thought that if I got divorced, I had failed.

Access tools and processes assist you in gaining and following your awareness. I couldn't stuff my awareness that the relationship wasn't really working for me anymore. It was too painful. I started to realize how much of me I had been cutting off to make the relationship work. I began to choose more of what I truly desired. The more I changed, the more I realized, "You know what? This doesn't really work for me!" So I used the tools to allow us to separate in the kindest way possible.

What if separating didn't have to come from the anger, force, hurt and, upset associated with most break-ups? What if it were simply a choice? Sometimes relationships run their course. At first, I didn't want to acknowledge this for myself and wouldn't even look at it. All of my justifications would come up: My parents divorced. I decided I would never get divorced. I hated that word, DIVORCE. I liked being married. We had two young kids. I didn't want to be a single mom. It was admitting failure.

Notice there were no questions in that mess? There were judgments, decisions I had made as a kid, and conflicting points of view. It took me five years before I was willing to ask questions about leaving my relationship. I was afraid to look into the future. But eventually, I got to the point where I just had to jump. If I stayed married, what would my life be like? If I got divorced, what would my life be like?

I learned how to expand my awareness of a choice into the future to sense what that choice would create. I played with this tool, looking at different aspects. If I chose to leave the relationship, what would it be like for me, for my children, for my ex-husband, for the family.... Each question brought an immediate awareness of expansion. Was that possible?!

I believed other people's points of view. Divorce was wrong, a bad thing, a failure that led to devastation for most, especially the children. (Although from my point of view, I turned out ok. I could even see the blessing in my parent's choice to split up.) I pulled in all the courage I could muster and started asking questions. Each time I looked into each future, it was much more expansive to move on than to stay married. Weird. Different than I had imagined. When something doesn't work for you, or your relationship doesn't work for you, it does not mean it's a failure! As soon as I made the choice, I had a talk with my husband and acknowledged that the relationship was not working. There was so much relief in both of our worlds. It felt like a huge weight was lifted.

Everywhere you've made yourself a failure because a relationship isn't working, or didn't work, or wherever you have tried to bend, fold, staple and mutilate yourself to make it work, and it still doesn't work, and you're making yourself wrong for it, will you let that go and consider other possibilities, please?

Asking questions allows you to begin perceiving different possibilities you will never know if you don't ask. That's the difficulty with deciding something—whatever you decide, you are right. And you are stuck. It is a conclusion. There is nothing else possible from your point of view. If something doesn't work, OK, acknowledge you're stuck and ask questions like: "What else is possible®?" "What would my life be like if we made a different choice?" "What if we separated or divorced?" "What would it be like for the kids?" "What would it create for my partner?"

If it is clear that moving on is your choice, ask "How can we move forward in a way that doesn't include judgment?" What if you could just look at and observe what is, what works, and what doesn't work? There is so much ease and space in those questions. Moving forward could be (and should be) an expansive, joyful adventure.

I'm not saying the transition will have no challenges; you will be challenged. You may even doubt your choice. Although our divorce was smooth and easy, afterward we did hit some bumps and some huge rough patches. When difficulties came up, my favorite tool was getting my Bars run. Access Bars® free you from the stuck feeling of no-choice. The Bars are a light touch energetic healing process done on the head that relaxes your entire body, clears mind chatter, and allows you to feel more space and clarity. It cleared away all of the upset so that I could deal with the situation from a space of observation, rather than judgment. It takes practice to trust yourself. Keep asking, keep choosing, and you will find things getting much better.

After the divorce, I went through a period of dating. During this time, I realized I was trying to heal every man I would date! With each person I would meet, I had so much awareness that I could fix this; I could handle that; I could help them with this—it was all one directional toward them. It was as if I had blended a request for clients with a request for dates. That was a fascinating awareness for me.

Someone to fix was not exactly the kind of person I wanted to date. That wasn't the greatest way to create a relationship. How many of you have done that? How many of you have found someone (or many) to create a relationship with and to heal? Or, have you chosen someone you know you could heal, but you also know that they won't receive from you, so it is hard work, backfires, and you're still a failure?! Sound familiar?

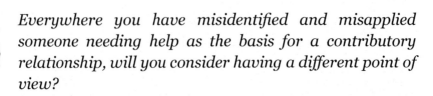

Everywhere you have misidentified and misapplied someone needing help as the basis for a contributory relationship, will you consider having a different point of view?

Funny how we choose the fixer-uppers because it gives us something to dig into and work at; it makes you feel like you're doing something of value. But once I started to realize, OK that doesn't work well, and this other thing didn't work either, I started to ask, "OK what is it I would like?" Keep asking questions!

Being untangled from your past relationships and having clarity of what you'd like is key. Each choice I made gave me more awareness. Probably the greatest choice I made was to take a period of 6-12 months to be single and commit to me, rather than go (jumping) into a relationship. I still went out and met people, but rather than tripping into thoughts about what it could be like with each new man, I enjoyed one date and learned a lot about myself. I learned what my priorities were, what I desired, and what it was like to have my own back.

I recommend spending some time with yourself. Start to get some clarity on what you would like, looking at the elements that you desire to have in a relationship. Also, take time to look at the things that don't work for you. And start to get a sense of what it would be like to have somebody in your life who is a contribution to you. A contributory relationship is where the person does not become your life but adds to your life, and you add to theirs.

One day, about nine months after I made the commitment to myself, I headed to a cafe before I went for a walk in the deep redwoods. On my way in to order an espresso, I sensed an energy that caught my attention and became aware of a man in front of me in line. He was in bike gear from head-to-toe, including helmet and glasses. Not looking to meet anyone, just being aware of people around me, I exchanged a few words with him, and he rode off.

As I read my book and sipped my espresso, I was content. The hike which followed was exhilarating; I loved connecting with the earth, feeling the peace and expansiveness of the trees. All the while I could feel the presence of the man I had just met. I didn't know his name, but I felt his energy. We ran into each other a few days later at the same cafe. "How was your ride?" I asked. He responded, "You should know; I took you with me. You were the wind blowing gently at my back all the way home as tears streamed down my face." Connections like this are possible. We just need to be aware of when those energies are present.

Begin looking at some general energies of what would be kind to you. What would be nurturing to you and your body, what would be fun for you, and what would it be like to experience those energies in your life coming from wherever and whomever? As you ask and allow yourself to receive, and even gift those energies to yourself, you start to attract a different kind of person. And you can begin to recognize if the people coming to you match the energies you are looking for, or not. Listen to *your* whispers of knowing.

This chapter is a short introduction to *Committing to YOUR Life: Conscious Coupling & Uncoupling.* I have created an Energy Therapy practice to facilitate others going through difficulties in their relationships. Together we look at and acknowledge what is working and where things need to change. Whether couples stay together or break up is totally their choice; they work with me to unwind from the stress that has built up over time, and gain the clarity they seek to start creating a relationship that works for each of them.

I would love to hear from you to see what you'd like to know about, what you're dealing with, what is sticking you. What tools and processes can I share with you to make your transitions easier and give you the greatest benefit? Connect with me at www.JulieTutonEnergy.com for some free downloads and tools, and to schedule a session. What is possible with Committing to Your Life that you'd love to create?!

About the Author
Julie Tuton

Best Selling Author, Energy Therapist & Certified Facilitator of Access Consciousness, as well as artist & jewelry designer, Julie Tuton has been creating magic with and for her clients over three decades.

Hailing from Boston, Julie has an East Coast edge, softened by years of living in the San Francisco Bay Area. She has a razor sharp awareness that allows her to cut through to the core of your issues with the kindness and caring you have always wished for but never found.

Perhaps it's because she comes from a place of non-judgment, Julie is real with you. Applying her awareness and practical tools to facilitate each of these transitions, she knows what you are going through. She comes from a place of vulnerability, compassion, and knowing that if she could move through life's transitions with ease, she can facilitate others as well.

Find Julie at:

www.JulieTutonEnergy.com
www.JulieTuton.com

Loving is a Pretty Interesting Art

BY JULIA SOTAS

Loving is a pretty interesting art. Sometimes you find the most beautiful things in the most unlikely places. That's what Anthony was for me. When I first met him at an Access Consciousness® class in Costa Rica, I saw him as a sweet, good-looking father of three. I had no idea the kindness that was beyond his exterior. But at that time, it would have been impossible for me to receive because I wasn't receiving the beauty of my own being yet.

When I was a little girl, I somehow knew that I came here for a special reason. I never told a soul, for fear that they would demolish it with their judgments. The secret I guarded so well was that I knew that I could love in a way that nobody had loved before. I could love with a sweetness and kindness and vulnerability that was unique to me—my own special way that had not been seen here yet.

I really enjoy dating. I love experimenting and learning about people, and love that the way they function changes my life in different ways. I don't believe in "the one," but when I met Anthony he was like an ingredient that added to the recipe of my life, a recipe that had been great before, yet became phenomenal with the last ingredient.

Anthony and I have an unconventional way of being together in the world. He is really vulnerable and willing to go places that I have never known another man to go. Sometimes I wonder how I was able to create a relationship that works so well for me, and then I realize I had cultivated an intense intimacy with myself prior to meeting him.

When I started taking Access Consciousness classes, the founder, Gary Douglas would constantly poke at me, telling me that I couldn't get anything accomplished in my life because I was waiting for Prince Charming to find me. I would get so frustrated when I would ask him a question about my business, and he would completely evade it and say, "You don't like business, you're sitting around waiting for a man to take care of your business." I fought him left, right and center. I did everything in my power to prove that I could create my life.

As I allowed his ideas to permeate my life, I began to think about the concept of relationship and how we are taught to find one person to build a life with. I began to wonder what it would be like if, instead of doing relationship, you did oneness, which would allow you to create your life, your future, and your home with the entire universe rather than with just one person. You can build a life with one person, and it can create something nice, or you will get divorced, or whatever; it's not a wrong choice. Often when we get married, without realizing it, we begin to exclude the contribution from other sources. We act and conclude that we have to be a certain way. A friend of mine used to have a massage therapist who was incredibly nurturing to her body. She really enjoyed going to him. At one point, the massages changed completely. He was no longer being the kind, nurturing energies with her that he had been before. Because he had gotten back together with his ex-partner, he didn't allow himself to gift and receive with my friend the way he had in the past.

What if you let yourself create your life with the universe instead cutting yourself off from all the energies and possibilities available by only including one person in your life? What if your choices didn't have to be in the hands of just you and your partner? What if the choices you make could include the awareness and contribution of the whole universe? How much magic could live in each choice?

Being alone was an amazing thing to cultivate. It took quite a while to unhook myself from the need for a relationship before I could cultivate the willingness to be alone. I finally made a choice one day that I had to live alone, away from my parents and friends. I made arrangements to move 1200 miles across the country and take on an apartment a little above my budget. Doing this gave me the space to create a life beyond the expectations other people had of me. For the first time, I began to realize my own points of view, beyond what my parents and friends thought, and outside of the mentality of my home province. I wasn't having average anymore. I began to feel what it could be like to be wealthy, and I gave myself permission to have the best. Everything else in my life improved to match my choice.

One week after I made the choice to move to Vancouver, I began to know Anthony in a new way. He told me that the first time he met me he knew the magic that was possible between us. He had previously made attempts to connect, but I was completely uninterested. I thought that I might break the heart of somebody really sweet, and I didn't want to do that to him, so I didn't let him in.

Anthony asked me if I wanted my Bars® run. I responded, "Okay, fine, but no kissing." He said, "Okay, okay." So he came to my room, and I could feel the way he was touching my head. There was something so different about it, almost like the way you would imagine a mama bird would hold her baby eggs. I had never felt anything so soft and caring in all my life; except for the softness of the touch I was cultivating for myself through the willingness to be alone and to create my life regardless of who else was in it or not.

I had decided that I was going to be happy being an aunt, a bridesmaid, and a friend. Having a husband or children was not something I needed anymore. I almost felt I didn't need a relationship with anyone else because my relationship with myself was so beautiful. I could be alone for days and love every second of it. I laughed by myself at my jokes and was happy to do so. I took myself out for nice dinners and a glass of wine. Once I sat in the best seat in the house at a table for four overlooking the ocean in downtown Vancouver during a very busy Saturday night. People stared at me angrily waiting for my party to arrive and I reveled in the fact that my party was already there. A party of me.

It was my time.

When Anthony touched me, I had never been touched that way before. The softness of it absolutely blew me away. I had no idea what to do with it. Eventually, we started kissing, and it was completely beyond anything I had known to be possible. As he started kissing me, clothes started coming off. I remember when he first held me naked. It was like every atom of my body was caressed with the kindness of the earth and the whole universe, as though he was the conduit. After we made love, he held me. He held me as long as I needed and he was so happy to do it. He just wanted to be close to my skin—close to me.

Afterward, he rolled over in bed and started talking about the time he had been spending with the founders of Access Consciousness, Gary Douglas and Dr. Dain Heer. I had never seen him like this. The being that came out was the funniest, most beautiful person I had ever seen.

After that night, we started getting closer. When it was finally time for me to move to Vancouver, he drove cross country with me and carried every box. He helped me unpack and he became very sad. I walked into my bedroom to find him hanging my clothes one by one. It was very intimate the way he touched each garment and how the straps confused him, but he did his best. I had never felt so taken care of before, by anyone other than myself.

Five years prior, Anthony's wife had taken her life due to severe bipolar and left him a single dad of three children. When I met him, his children were six, twelve, and fourteen. When he first asked me to go down to South Carolina and spend time with his family, my instant reaction was,

"No! I am not getting married; I am not having kids. I am going to be an auntie and a bridesmaid." I really cared for Anthony, so I asked what would be lightest: to go or not to go. Beyond a shadow of a doubt, it was lighter to go. So I went.

The first time I laid eyes on Anthony's children, I felt intense caring for each of them, but this caring frightened me. I was twenty-three, and his oldest was fourteen. The level of responsibility that I saw in front of me was overwhelming. At the same time, I had an amazing level of peace when I spent time with them. I stepped instantly into the role of the mother. It felt was so natural, it was surreal. But I kept having thoughts about how having an instant family would take me away from my preset dreams. It made me angry that I could have that level of caring for them, yet not be able to have everything else I desired. One of the things I learned from Access Consciousness is that when you are angry, it means there is a lie somewhere in the mix. I was angry at the lie that I could not have it all.

At first, I was a romantic; I spent my life waiting for someone to tell me I was the best. When I started listening to the words of Gary Douglas, I came to my own conclusion that love and consciousness could not coexist. This was not correct! When I connected with Anthony, I had to reconnect to my romantic side. He didn't allow me to deny it because he matched me so well.

I had the idea that business was spreading consciousness, and that I had to shut the door to Anthony and his kids in order to have a business or to do the work of consciousness. Only when I was done with that idea could I open the door to them again. I bought that there were two different worlds, one of business, money, and finances, and the other of the softness of the relationship, sex, my nurtured body, and children.

When I was first with Anthony, I dipped $30,000 into debt, and that arose from the point of view that I could have either love or money. When I chose love, my money was a disaster. I had to create something different, which required me to embrace the willingness to know that there are no parts and pieces of us. There are no categories. We can have softness in business. We can bring intensity into our relationship. We don't have to sacrifice one for the other. We can be everything that we are. It was a really intense awareness for me.

Sometimes to get to the spaces of vulnerability during sex, dark energies come up, and you have to be willing to look them in the eye and bypass them or destroy and uncreate them. It is a deeply uncomfortable level of receiving. It takes courage beyond this reality to receive in that way. Most people have decided that being shut down and having barriers is the only way to keep themselves safe. There are so many energies we are taught or entrained to hide from, including depression, abuse, aloneness. To truly receive from yourself and others, you have to really be willing to put your barriers down and possibly even go through all the uncomfortable energies. You actually have to put your walls down and face all of that to create a phenomenal relationship.

I am very much a woman in that I do a lot of subtext and a lot of meanness to men. If you pay attention, you'll see that women put men down quite often. I could be really mean to Anthony in the beginning, and sometimes I still find it coming out. When I recognize myself doing this, I ask, "What other energies do I have available?" so I can choose a different way of being.

When people are around Anthony and me, they say there is something different about us. Our friends are delighted when we walk into the room together because we create a certain magic by putting our two beings together. My point of view is that if you are going to have a relationship, only be in it if it will make your life ten times greater than if you were on your own. I'm not even willing to have a relationship that makes my life five times greater. It's not about finding "an Anthony" or even about which man you choose. It's about asking yourself, "What am I willing to receive? How vulnerable am I willing to be?"

What Anthony and I have is a result of intense intimacy with self. You cannot set out searching for a relationship; you must set out searching for intimacy with yourself. A relationship may stumble into your life afterward, but never from the need of relationship, only from the addition that will create the most magic in your life.

About the Author
Julia Sotas

Julia Sotas has always been on the quest for total consciousness. Since she was a child, she had her nose buried books such as *The Power of Your Subconscious Mind* and *The Power of Now*.

When she came across the tools of Access Consciousness as a young woman, it was love at first sight. Six years later, Julia travels the world attending and facilitating Access Consciousness classes on topics such as Love, Finances, The Earth and The Creation of a Totally New Reality on Planet Earth.

Julia holds a degree in Sociology from the University of Winnipeg, Canada. She currently resides in Bluffton, South Carolina, with her husband Anthony and their beautiful family.

You can find her weekly Podcast on iTunes at *Access with Julia.*

Settling for "Good Enough" Just About Killed Me

BY RHONDA BURNS

"He's a nice guy. He's the boy-next-door poster child. I won't be able to find anyone better."

Those were the words I uttered to myself when I said, "Yes" to my boyfriend's marriage proposal shortly after my college graduation. Although we had a great deal of fun together, I never felt the deep physical or emotional connection that I knew was vital in creating something long-lasting. So when I graduated from college and took a job away from the area, I surprised the crap out of myself when the proposal came and I said yes. You know, because "He's a nice guy and I won't be able to find anyone better." What does that tell you about the state of affairs this girl was in emotionally?

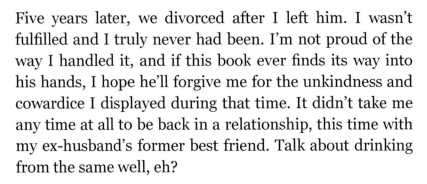

Five years later, we divorced after I left him. I wasn't fulfilled and I truly never had been. I'm not proud of the way I handled it, and if this book ever finds its way into his hands, I hope he'll forgive me for the unkindness and cowardice I displayed during that time. It didn't take me any time at all to be back in a relationship, this time with my ex-husband's former best friend. Talk about drinking from the same well, eh?

After two years of dating, I basically threatened my guy with, "Either you make a commitment and move this along, or I'm gone." What do you know, the engagement ring showed up! After two years of engagement, we finally took the leap. Our marriage was officiated by a purple-robed Merlin-the-Magician type man with a long, white beard at the Excalibur Hotel in Las Vegas, NV. As liberated as I felt at that time, and as much fun as we had, I can't help but think back on it all and shake my head. I may have been four years older and somewhat wiser, but if you drill down into it, I was the same person as before with only a slight variation on the theme.

Although my second husband and I lasted a total of 11 years together, we couldn't manage to keep the relationship train on the tracks. Hell, I don't know how we lasted as long as we did with the lack of skills we had between my controlling and emasculating tendencies and our inability to be truly vulnerable with each another. The scary thing about it is that we were a walking, talking model of every other couple in our circle of influence. The two greatest gifts that came from that marriage are my incredible son who manages to be one of my greatest teachers, and finding out just how capable I really am of changing things. To this day, my ex and I are friends. We co-parent from separate households, and we've managed to co-create a fantastic life for our son—apart. For that, I am truly grateful, and I appreciate everything we've accomplished thus far.

When I left my second marriage, (again, my choice) I began a more in-depth journey into me and tried to determine why I was really here and what all my choices were really about. For a while, I felt like a pinball banging around inside a pinball machine. I would float (or shoot) from one dating scenario to the next, each guy and relationship seemingly moving me one step closer to what I thought I was looking for with each choice. It was a slow and painful process at times! I was constantly asking myself what was wrong with me. Here I was, a successful, intelligent, attractive, funny, and adventurous woman, yet I kept attracting guys who weren't willing to commit, or only wanted to engage in something physical. On the opposite end of the spectrum, I attracted guys who were ready to lock it down and marry me within of a matter of days or weeks!

Somehow, I did manage to create a sane, enjoyable two-year relationship with a kind and generous man about three-and-a-half years after my divorce was final. It was during this time that I was introduced to a body of work that literally altered my universe. I had been a continual seeker; a personal development junkie, always reading self-help books, attending seminars and classes, and I even changed career tracks to move from corporate America into a professional coaching career. I wasn't at a loss for "information" on how to do relationship, where I'd gone wrong, or how to get it right. What was different about this

body of work is that its overall target is to empower people to know that they know.

Every other system or product out there seems to be great at telling you what you should or shouldn't do, say, or be. This body of work encourages YOU to know; to ask questions, and to make choices to gain awareness. I was like a kid in a candy store, and I was eating it up. What the work of Access Consciousness® showed me is that I really was doing the best I could based on what I was modeled, shown, and had learned or mimicked. It also showed me the millions of ways I was judging every aspect of me, my choices, my relationships, my points of view, and my beliefs in every moment and from every angle.

For much of my life, I functioned from the role of the eternal caregiver. I tended to everyone's needs first and foremost, ensuring all were happy. Then if I got around to it, I could take care of me. This usually didn't happen until I was so run down, resentful and angry that I couldn't help but explode like a raging volcano, and then find a way to excuse myself (guiltily and shamefully) so that I could recharge my batteries. It was an ugly, vicious cycle that went on for many, many years, and the stress it put on both my body and psyche, as well as on those I love and care for almost brings me to tears. I also functioned (unknowingly) 100% from the point of view that I *had* to be in a relationship. I didn't know how NOT to be in a relationship. As "successful" as I was in the other areas of my life, knowing what an absolute mess my relationships were left me feeling like an utter fraud as a woman, lover, wife, daughter, sister, and human being.

Absolutely, without question, I know these things to be true: we honestly do the best we can with what we've got and with what we've learned. I've also come to know, beyond a shadow of a doubt, that ANYTHING truly IS changeable. I'm a walking, talking example of it, as are a slew of friends and peers I've met in recent years. The key is, you have to be willing to know this. No, you probably won't know how something may come to be, or when, or what it will be like, or how much it might cost, or even what it might require of you, but you must be willing to believe that ANYTHING is changeable. That's it. Just be willing.

Would you be willing to take it from someone like me? After all, I have two failed marriages under my belt and countless tear-filled hours of anguish. Add to that, thousands of online dating email exchanges, too many mediocre dates to count, and endless numbers of emotional ties to the past I couldn't let go of. Throw in constant cries and prayers to God to help me be a less of a loser (obviously, since I couldn't get any of this right). Get the point? Now, standing on the other side of that trauma and drama, I'm creating a life and living I can claim and own proudly. YES, this is the life I always knew was possible! It's the one I've always desired for myself. If I can do it, honey, believe me, you can too.

I never speak words I don't mean (trust me on this or check in with those who know me best), and I certainly wouldn't ask anyone to do something I hadn't either tried or would be willing to try myself. I not only talk the talk, friends—I walk it. Sometimes the walk is a limp, or bruised and sore, but I walk it. And I have the utmost respect for those mentors and leaders I've had the honor and pleasure to learn from who do the same. People talk a great game sometimes, and with the advent of the internet, we have the ability to get almost any bit of information we could ever ask for. With any potential teachers, or anyone you desire to learn from, would you be willing to ask, "Are they speaking from a place of experience, authenticity, and genuine desire to pay it forward?"

While I love to share stories and experiences with people, what I really love to do (and feel I'm built for) is to utilize my experience and tools to empower, equip, and invite people to a) show up in their lives in ways they may never have even dreamed was possible, and b) to be the greatest, most genuine "them" they can possibly be—whatever that looks like. How better to do this than to share the tools I know and love, as well as to offer personal experience with what has assisted me to realize an unshakable strength, grit, and determination that I didn't even know I had. The power and the tenacity I function from now come from an immensely deep well of vulnerability, kindness, and caring that has always been there. Now I actually tap into it to benefit myself and others, instead of benefitting others while ignoring me.

If I could share anything with you, it would be this: When you are willing to make a demand to trust and to know Y-O-U totally, fully, and wholly, you become an unstoppable and rare force in the world. As much as I thought I wanted a relationship, or that I was supposed to be in one because that's the way the world expects us to be, when I tapped into what was real and true for me in any given moment, I realized that I actually wanted to become able to be comfortable by myself—and in my own skin; to not have to be in relationship out of some feeling of necessity or obligation, or in order to fit in.

It has been over three years since my last relationship, and in that time, I've been able to accomplish just that. Some days have been easier than others. It was during the days and nights that I was alone with my feelings of despair, or with emotions that welled up from a really deep space, that I realized all the times I hadn't acknowledged or addressed that they were even there. And I hadn't given the time and attention to those feelings and emotions so that they could change, or be released entirely.

Staying in the space of the discomfort, the pain, the emotions, and the difficulty allowed me to give a voice to what needed to be spoken. Even if just to me, I gave words to the unknown, a voice, and an outlet. In doing so, I was able to let them go. They don't run the show anymore. They don't secretly sabotage my desire for creating connection with people in any type of relationship. Standing in the hottest, most fiery parts of myself, I learned that I didn't burn; I didn't die—if anything, I came out of those flames clearer, more unencumbered and more real than I believed I could be. I don't have the need to "prove" my worth or my value to anyone anymore. If I take care of people now, it's from a genuine desire, simply because it brings me joy to do so. I don't have to pretend to be someone I'm not, nor do I have to do anything perfectly or "right." These were all patterns that were deeply ingrained and that I had entrained to, and I held tightly to them for the majority of my life. I'm actually willing to fail miserably, muck things up royally, and to be judged as wrong or terrible now. Talk about freedom and happiness...yeah, more than I ever dreamed was possible.

How'd I get to this place, you may wonder? I'd love to share with you. These are simple, pragmatic tools/tips/practices you can use, beginning right now, if you choose. What I know about these tools is that they work—when you work them. Having a full tool box and not using the tools to create more clarity, ease, freedom, and joy is like trying to build a house without a hammer, nails, saws, and the like. Tools make things better and easier. They can help the changes come with more speed than you might imagine. You will also have to be willing to do things different if you want different results. Got it? If something is not working for you, do something different! Things not shifting or changing? Ask a different question. Your willingness to be and do different, even to a minor degree, can catalyze results that could make your head spin!

Make the demand of yourself to TRUST YOU—no matter what. My demand was, "I don't care what it takes, I'm going to trust me, my intuition, and my knowing—first and foremost. I don't care how ridiculous my awareness may seem in the moment; if it's light and true for me, I'm going to trust it and go with it. Period."

Be PRESENT in your life at all times. The majority of the world stays "checked out" or removed from their day-to-day lives for various reasons. If you aren't willing to be present in your life in every moment, you aren't going to get all the information and awareness that can assist you in creating exactly what you want and removing what you don't. It's as simple as asking yourself, "Am I 100%

present right now? Where did I just go? What is the value of checking out or being absent?"

Write down a list of what you say you want. It can be a broad list pertaining to your whole life, or can focus specifically on relationships. Write it ALL down. Go through each line, one by one, and ask yourself, "Truth, is this my want/wish/desire?" If it doesn't light you up, make you happy, and totally feel like a big fat "YES!" when you ask, scratch through it and move to the next. So much of what we decide we want is based on what we see others choosing or what the "norm" is in society, and we just naturally fall in line. This exercise allows us to get clear on what belongs to us and what doesn't.

Go through your remaining list and ACKNOWLEDGE what is there. We can't actually have something or have it change if we don't acknowledge it in the first place. It's as simple as saying, "Yes, I desire to create and have _____." Own it.

Once you've acknowledged your desires, ASK for them. "Universe (or whatever you deem as your higher power/God/source/etc.), I'd love to have _____ show up! I wonder what it might be like when it does?" Stay in the space of playful curiosity with your request, and then let it go. Once you've written it down, acknowledged it, and asked, it's in the mix, and there's no reason or necessity to chase it. This is where the magic begins. If you are like me, and sometimes think you're in control of when and how things show up, it may be a process of learning to trust the Universe. It has NEVER let me down. NEVER. As a bonus, you can continue to ask for more and more possibilities—

there is NO end to the "ask and receive" process. It's an abundant universe!

If you don't know what you want, shop around. Be willing to try on different things to see if they light you up, or not. Gary M. Douglas, the founder of Access Consciousness, calls this "shopping for your reality." How do we know what we desire if we aren't looking, listening, considering, or trying things on for size? And just because you find something that seems like a fit now, it doesn't mean you have to keep it or choose it forever. Nope, just for the time that it suits you!

Finally, be willing to BE and DO whatever it takes. If you say you want something, are you willing to make the demand of yourself to create it? If not, how will the Universe believe you? If you aren't committed to you, your life, and having what you desire, the uncertainty will slow it down, if not stop it altogether. Be a wide-open channel and a clear magnet.

May these tools contribute dynamically to you and may your life be everything you desire it to be—and more!

About the Author
R h o n d a   B u r n s

Rhonda Burns is champion coach and success catalyst with a "definitely different" perspective on life, living, and everything else. As a dynamic professionally certified global coach, as well as a popular inspirational speaker, intuitive wellness facilitator, writer, and weekly radio show host, Rhonda motivates, catalyzes, facilitates, empowers and mentors clients using undeniable warmth and extensive humor.

Utilizing curiosity, playfulness, joy, and ease, Rhonda's vibrant and exuberant personality coupled with the space of no judgment not only invites people into the fullness and truth of themselves but also provides the catalyzing energy to quicken the time frame, allowing them to achieve their greatest levels of success, faster.

A natural illuminator, status-quo disruptor, and perspective-shifter, Rhonda skillfully moves clients through and out of limiting points of view with lightning speed and laser-like clarity. A single mother, entrepreneur, adventurer, and former Fortune 500 national sales professional, Rhonda successfully and abundantly thrives in every endeavor.

As a tenacious continual seeker of more awareness who enjoys creating change and unraveling all the limitations she had created and adopted for herself over her lifetime, Rhonda has traveled the pitted and rutted roads that many of her clients are traveling. She has "been there and done that," and desires to assist others in shortening their roads and in creating much more ease with a whole lot more fun on the journey.

With years of formal education, personal and professional development, extensive "real-life" skills, professional expertise, certified coaching training, a varied and diverse array of dynamic and pragmatic tools, Rhonda works with clients who seek deeper meaning, deeper truth, and have an unwavering desire to show up in the world as the truest, greatest expression of themselves. In short, she helps them to live their most vibrant, extraordinary lives.

Rhonda works selectively with bold, committed clients that have a "no-matter-what-it-takes" attitude to claim, create, and implement the lives that most aren't willing to go for. If you're looking to be celebrated and supported as a savvy woman who wants to Rock the Motherload with guts & grace, please join her on Facebook on the Rock the Motherload™ page. You can find out more by visiting www.rhonda-burns.com or www.rockthemotherload.com.

RELATIONSHIPS
Done Easy

Also, feel free to join Rhonda each week on her radio show, *Rock the Motherload,* formerly the *Potency Is My Game!* Radio show on inspiredchoicesnetwork.com. All shows are archived for replay there, as well as on iTunes.

Delicious We

BEING THE LUSCIOUS LEADER OF YOUR LOVE LIFE

BY DANNA LEWIS

This man who sits sweetly next to me at restaurants; snuggles up against me at night making sure some part of his body is touching mine; sidles up behind me to feast on my neck; kisses me tenderly on the forehead and touches me with more kindness and desire than I ever perceived possible, is a gift in my life beyond my imaginings. That he gazes at me with such adoration, admiration, and gratitude that it melts me into a puddle of yum is somewhat bewildering at times, humbling at others, and most often an acknowledgment that inspires an innate sense of knowing within me. This knowing comes from the demand I have made to have a relationship different from anything I had seen in childhood, and different from anything I had encountered throughout most of my life. I desired a romantic relationship that would be a constant demand for greater: loving and kind; potent and sweet; adoring and appreciating; sexy and sensual yet warm, nurturing, and rejuvenating. I craved a connection that was forgiving and empowering, one that continually pushed my edges of receiving, inviting me to my best self while tugging at the threads of consciousness that disintegrate the walls of limitation.

I'm not exactly sure when I asked the Universe to deliver this gift of intimately expansive possibilities. It wasn't any particularly big "aha" moment—more like a million small moments that always became the energetic question, "What else is possible?®" I knew something else was possible at three when my father pushed my mother down the stairs. I knew something else was possible at age five when my mother would leave in the middle of the night to go to a domestic violence shelter. I knew something else was possible at seven when my brother and I called 911 so the police would come put a stop to the violence and screaming. I knew something else was possible during all those romantic comedies in which major drama and trauma climaxed into a kiss that alluded to "happily ever after" and during all those years of sitcoms where the women bashed and emasculated the men.

I had watched people I knew make choices that contracted and destroyed their connection with their partners, under the guise of "this is the way relationships are." Throughout all my years of dating, mini-relationships, first marriage, divorce, and my return to dating life in San Francisco where I live, I knew for sure that "the something else" had to come from me choosing to lead my life and create my relationship in a different way.

Along the way, I've learned that your willingness to choose is the greatest power you have. That said, when you're not yet able to choose, the resources of consciousness are the most dynamic and transformational tools on the planet. The work of Access Consciousness® has gifted me priceless information that has eliminated almost all of my PTSD, clearing destructive patterns and limiting points of view, while providing the generative tools and techniques I required to create the something greater than I knew was available. I am boundlessly grateful to the creators of Access, Gary Douglas and Dr. Dain Heer, for their pioneering, benevolent, and tenacious work and contribution to consciousness.

Delicious We Relationship Tip #1

Your relationship is in "creation mode" long before your person shows up. Every time I knew something else was possible, I was creating the relationship I have today. Every time I went on a date and got an awareness of what would work for me, I was creating the relationship I have today. A useful tool for this is to acknowledge and claim these things for yourself with a "Yes. I'll have that." And be clear on what doesn't work for you.

I remember the moment I saw my boyfriend Rob's picture on the online dating site that brought us together. My whole body and being perceived his energy, then I heard a little whisper in my head that said, "I want to snuggle with that man." We quickly set up a date to meet, but I postponed that first date and almost canceled completely. The reasons—my cat was sick, my business was not where I thought it should be, I had just been on a few weird and not particularly fun dates—were no match for the energetic pull that got me to that first date three nights later. When our eyes met and I smiled at him, I watched his entire universe shift, and I knew I would recall that look on his face for the rest of my life.

Somewhere between our first and second dates, this thing we call "our relationship" morphed into its own consciousness. I could perceive that consciousness (and still do) with more ease and vulnerability than anything I've experienced so far. It's like a psychic connection with a child, knowing what it needs—food, water, rest, energy for growth, attention, affection, space, quiet time, creative activities—at any given moment and being able to respond, engage, and interact with ease.

Delicious We Relationship Tip #2

Treat your relationship as a threesome! The following questions will allow you to honor your partner, you, and the relationship. What does my partner require and desire of me today? What do I require and desire of me in this relationship today? What does the relationship require and desire today? Playing with these awarenesses can add so much more ease in creating, enjoying and sparking inspired actions in your relationship.

There was a two-week lapse between our first and second date because Rob was out of town on business. Because he is a chef, I watched the movie *Chef* to have something to text and chat with him about. We could look at that as a girly moment of insecurity or a brilliant awareness of what could create more. He was then moved to watch the movie, and it inspired our second date location. En route to that date (in separate cars), a calamity of events including a parade and a restaurant that ran out of food resulted in a new plan where I would swing by to pick him up, and we would find a restaurant together. Once we had been driving together for several blocks, I heard another whisper of awareness: "Get out of the car and hug him." And then a doubt. "Really? We've only seen each other once; there's traffic; why do I have to be the one do it?"

So there I was, pulling over on a busy street corner, getting out of my car and hugging a man I had only met once before. Our hugs have become a famous and sometimes infamous, yet integral action in our connection, communion, and clearing of crap. From that first hug, every time Rob and I would come together I would inquire where my hug was, and as he will agree, literally stand stubbornly in front of him and demand one. Our hugs are full-on, wrapped around each other as long as it takes for the density, electrical charge, and chaos of life to dissipate into blissful, acoustical spaciousness. When things are great with us, it's a super juicy connecting "hello" to our beings and bodies. When one of us is out of sorts, the hug allows the other person to contribute an energy of loving kindness, nurturing, and appreciation, washing away the day's stress and struggle. When something is going on in our relationship, a hug has often been the potently silent game-changer that shifts us forward to loving kindness without ever having to talk things out, hash things over or analyze a situation. How does it get any better than that?®

Delicious We Relationship Tip #3

Be tenacious with your awareness. My choice to listen to that one whisper of awareness and be the initiator of our hugs invited one of our relationship's greatest tools of loving kindness and generative space. My tenacity and sometimes OCD belligerence in demanding, while not always graceful, has always created more. And what I secretly love most about this? If I'm prissy or pissy, Rob's demand of our hug shifts the space. It is an extremely tangible acknowledgment of the influence for greater that I am, and actionable gratitude he is for his own knowing.

Speaking of gratitude... the day the "L" word was spoken out loud, all hell broke loose! Actually, it was consciousness that broke loose, and I'm forever grateful to myself for having the gumption to respond the way I did. We were sitting side by side in a restaurant, and Rob started speaking softly about his feelings and reaching for words to express what we had been creating. He progressed from "I have these strong feelings for you that have been growing," to "I'm falling for you," to "I love you and am in love with you" in the speed of space. I was sitting quietly, graciously being with this man that I'd known (in this lifetime) for a very short period. I had a sense of how scary and vulnerable and exciting this is for anyone and especially for this man who was inviting me into his world after his experiences of heartbreak, loss, and choosing to create something greater for himself.

I think I may have been holding my breath. I was definitely pondering how I was going to get from his declaration to what I know is a bigger creator of relationship than love. So when he finished and almost shyly asked me if I was okay with him falling in love with me, I was silently thinking, "Yes, beautiful man, I am beyond okay with you falling in love with me and acknowledging the love that is growing between us." Out loud I said, "Can we please talk about gratitude now? And what love means to you? There are a million different meanings and judgments and definitions of what love is to any one person and when two people come together with their mountains of meanings and judgments and definitions about love, some conversation needs to occur. And, can you perceive the energy of gratitude we have for each other, for what we've been generating and what we can create together? That doesn't require any conversation; it just is." And then I continued, "This whole 'I love you' thing is just the beginning. Would you be willing to function from loving actions more than the conclusion of, 'I love you, we're together now?'" That's when my boyfriend looked at me with a look that makes me giddy; one that I have come to know, which communicates, "Who are you and how did I get so lucky to have you in my life?" And just like magic, our love and gratitude expanded even more.

Delicious We Relationship Tip #4

Gratitude and loving actions create the "yum!" Gratitude inherently generates expansion and ease because judgment (contraction) cannot exist in the space of gratitude. Here are some "gratitude kickstarters": What are three things you're grateful for about your partner? What are three things you're grateful for in your relationship? What are three things you are grateful for about you in your relationship? I've noticed that choosing this when I'm challenged (aka "in judgment"), begins to dissipate any contraction that was creating the irritation or aggravation.

(For 10 Delicious We Relationship Tips and my corresponding Luscious Leadership Life-Hacks go to http://www.dannalewis.com/deliciouswehacks or

Where do you begin in the evolving creation and consciousness of a relationship so that it is a joyful playground of infinitely expansive possibilities? Let's begin with how you start and end your day with your partner. My childhood experiences have driven me to create something sweet, loving, nurturing, and peaceful for our time together. I've been known to set my alarm early so I can wake up first, which gives me space to snuggle in with Rob and awaken him to a shower of kisses and love. We'll go for walks in the neighborhood before going to work. He might prepare my coffee cup with lots of sugar or make us breakfast. Or I might make his hand-poured coffee while he's in the shower. Other times he'll claim five more minutes for us, and we'll crawl back under the covers! If I'm on the phone when he's about to leave, I always put my conversation on pause for a moment to look him in the eye and kiss him goodbye. These may be small gestures, but the big love they create is vastly palpable. Watching my boyfriend walk into the world for the day with a smile on his face and in his heart is priceless.

That energy ripples out to everyone in our sphere of influence. Other random, playful, loving actions for us include always kissing each other goodnight; protecting our date night as much as possible; baking pies and playing games together, often with a sexy spin like "sexual favor" poker. That in itself has expanded my world and shown me where I hadn't been willing to ask for what I would like, which was limiting my receiving. Thank you, boyfriend, for being so open and willing to ask for what you desire, and joyfully giving me whatever I sometimes stumble in asking for. When we watch movies, he'll run my Bars (an energetic healing technique of Access Consciousness), and when we are snuggled up in bed, I'll run some of the Access energetic body processes. The energy work of Access has contributed nurturing, peaceful energies of communion to our relationship. And, every month we're together we take turns asking the other if he/she would still like to be the other's boyfriend/girlfriend. This creates a pause to be present, look at the energy and our future possibilities together.

What I love about these things is that we have a framework for loving actions, not a set structure. I'll admit that I have a harder time than Rob does if we don't take time for nurturing or playful interaction. This is where the rubber meets the road for me in clearing the issues of PTSD and childhood trauma. There's a place in me that has so much allowance and flexibility, mixed with the knowing of what choosing these things can create—though I still have trigger points that send me spinning. There are also things that trigger my boyfriend, pushing him too far past his edge of presence and into his check-out point. It has changed so much for me that we are willing to provide each other with valuable information about our triggers, and have the vulnerability and openness to acknowledge this and look at it with no judgment.

Whenever something would come up during the first few months of our relationship, I was adamant about not sharing it with Rob. I would turn inward, analyzing, dissecting, clearing every possible limiting belief I could discern to finally create a change for myself. Then, and only then, would I share any of it with him if I knew it would be a contribution to us. He told me that it was painful for him to watch as I went into stoic introspectiveness. At one point, this flipped, and I started sharing everything, bulldozing him with consciousness and my awareness. Since then, I've learned to employ the energy of "interesting point of view." This is a great Access Consciousness tool. It creates the space for question and choice, allowing us to look without judgment to discover if anything truly requires changing and if so, how to change it. We still talk about and through some things, it just has more relevance and expansion now.

When you do need a bitch session, do it with someone other than your partner! How kind and honoring is it to vomit all your thoughts, feelings, and emotions onto your partner? Being a conscious leader involves asking questions to gain awareness of what something will create. This reality's paradigm of making sure your partner knows and hears "your truth" is riddled with conclusions, projections, rejections, separations, and expectations. It can and often does create a lot of drama and trauma.

Change is an inevitable part of living and loving. Change to create something greater is a choice, and one I've discovered

I'm often willing to make. It is not always the easiest choice or the one that creates the smoothest moments! There are times when I know Rob would prefer I simply chill and not have everything be a constant question. He has asked me if having so much awareness and being so sensitive to everything going on around me is a burden. Yes, at times it can feel that way. Yet somewhere deep within my being, there is a vitality in knowing that consciousness is a gift. When our backgrounds, childhoods, previous relationships, and other people's impelled points of view have come crashing together it is my unyielding choice of consciousness, our willingness to be genuinely present with each other, to ask questions and always choose what will create greater that catapults our relationship into new realms. Those moments are pure gold when we both get it and tear up with gratitude for this dynamically powerful thing we are creating together. For Rob, those moments and those attributes are some of the things he admires, appreciates and acknowledges most about me and us.

With Rob, average will never do. What he creates daily in his kitchen as a master chef is pure magic. I showed up in his life because he was asking for something different. We share an intensity for luscious living, for being magic with our talents and capacities, and for always going for way beyond average...into inconceivable for some. This works deliciously well for us. We inspire each other daily. The enthusiasm we have for each other and our relationship boils down to choosing "delicious we" as the joyful playground of intimately expansive possibilities beyond what either of us has seen, experienced, or can perceive possible at times. I am so very grateful for him, for our relationship, and for the confidence, comfort, and generosity he has for letting me share our world with the world. Through this space of delicious we, I have come to know, trust, and appreciate myself as a leader—of not only my love life but my entire life. That continually pushes my edges of receiving and invites me to my best self while tugging at the threads of consciousness to disintegrate more walls of limitation to yet another space of beautiful being.

(For a recap of the 10 Delicious We Relationship Tips and my corresponding Luscious Leadership Life-Hacks go to http://www.dannalewis.com/deliciouswehacks).

About the Author
D a n n a   L e w i s

Danna Lewis is an Inspirational Speaker, Best-Selling Author, Consultant, Energy Healer and Success Coach for luscious leaders cultivating greatness from the bedroom to the boardroom. She has 20+ years of business experience, training, and certifications in consciousness and empowerment coaching. She educates and empowers executives, entrepreneurs and their teams to LEAD LUSCIOUSLY—with deep presence, strategic awareness, and courageous kindness to improve engagement, effectiveness, and enjoyment in the entire work-life spectrum. Business highlights include building high-performance work teams of happy, empowered employees on Wall Street; managing 400 million dollar bank accounts for the world's largest financial institution; creating multi-million dollar revenue streams in zero-sum revenue operation departments; and directing brand management and social media architecture for a luxury exercise franchise tripling in size during her tenure. She is trained in the Access Consciousness® and Joy of Business® modalities.

Her Luscious Leadership platform offers a variety of speaking topics, classes, workshops, and programs to provide pragmatic tools of mindfulness and conscious creation. Everything is targeted to gain higher levels of clarity; have creative control of your day, greatly reduce stress, trauma and drama; increase your bottom line; and have more joyful connection and contribution within the work life continuum. This is the creative edge of transformational work in exceeding desired results. Her clients appreciate the kindness, confidence, abundance of powerful information, and joyful creative energy she brings to the work.

Danna is a co-author in *The Energy of Receiving, The Energy of Creativity,* and this book, with several other book projects in the works. Her business career and company were preceded by a childhood wrought with domestic violence. Her tenacity and awareness of much greater possibilities have fueled her pioneering of learning about consciousness, exploring her hands-on healing capacities and creating a different reality for herself. She knows it is possible to thrive in all spaces of our lives and that by eliminating the artificial walls of limitation more contribution and receiving can exist; that levity, gratitude, and kindness can be incredibly potent forces of change; that choice and question always provide the possibilities to out-create anything. Danna currently lives with her executive chef boyfriend in San Francisco, CA during the week and their Monterey, CA home weekends with his seven year-old son.

Listen to Danna on her Luscious Leadership Radio Show at:

http://a2zen.fm/author/luscious-leadership/

Meet Danna and discover more about luscious leadership success coaching at www.dannalewis.com.

Relationship Done Differently

BY HANNA & JOAKIM VALDEVI

Ask and you shall receive

HANNA:

I desire an expansive, playful, nurturing communion with a caring, non-judgmental man. In 2010, I wrote this powerful desire in my notebook, without any bigger hope that it would come true. At the time, I had been in a 10-year relationship with the father of my three children. I knew that something had to change; I just hadn't wanted to admit it earlier. The relationship had become lame. I wasn't happy and neither was he. When I wrote down what I really desired, I did not conclude that I had to continue my relationship, or that I had to end it. I remember clearly thinking, *I'm willing to give this two more years.*

Almost two years later to the day, I met Joakim. I had decided at the last minute to attend a class that night. At the venue, I bounced up on a table, looked into the eyes of a young man who sat there looking lost, and joked with him in a surprisingly flirty way, "Do you come here often?" I didn't understand why I had asked; I was not normally flirty, and the young, long-haired, surfer-dude-wannabe wasn't really my type.

This story could have been over before it began if it wasn't for the fact that the universe had my back. It clearly knew that to get what I truly desired, the communication and choices had to be made through my body, NOT through my tirelessly computing brain. The class facilitator asked if I would give an energetic body process to a guy. It turned out to be the very guy I had flirted with earlier. "No problem," I said, totally unaware of the fact that this was one of those seemingly unimportant choices that would change my life completely!

A few minutes after I put my hands on his body, something happened that I could not put into words. A force that I had forgotten I had suddenly woke up within me. Vitality that I, for various reasons, had shut down during my childhood suddenly became present. In retrospect, I understand that it was the total sexualness (the healing, caring, nurturing, joyful, generative, expansive and orgasmic energy) that Joakim embodies that brought life back into my body. At that point, I just knew that this was an energy that I had missed throughout my adult life and that I wanted more of it. Strangely, this energy also brought me more of myself. And that, I couldn't get enough of.

JOAKIM:

I had just returned to Sweden after an unsuccessful attempt to move to Australia in the name of love. I think I knew early on that it wouldn't work out, but ignored my awareness, as I had so many times before. At this point, I began to feel discouraged when it came to relationships. There was always something missing or something wrong. I tried everything to get them to work, which usually separated me from myself and only made matters worse. I was tired of this cycle. *Maybe I wasn't made for relationships,* I thought. I had always been different. Then again, maybe there was nothing wrong with me. Maybe it was the way most people do relationship that didn't work for me. Maybe the way I *be* and what I value didn't fit in a normal relationship. I was delighted by this thought and deep in my heart I made a demand to the universe: *Either bring me the best relationship you've got, or I am not doing relationship!* My desire was completely honest. I was okay with not having a relationship and was also ready to have a completely different one. Excited and happy, I somehow knew that I just made a life-changing demand.

Two days later I met Hanna. She caught my attention as soon as she entered the room. There was something about the way she moved that was very appealing. Later when I asked the facilitator for an energetic body process, I somehow knew it would be that sexy girl who would gift me the process. When she placed her hands on my body, I felt like an instrument being played. The music was beautiful. Hanna ignited something within me that had been dormant for way too long—something that I always knew was possible but had stopped believing in.

Create - destroy and uncreate - re-create

HANNA:

When we started our relationship, I was determined to do it differently than any previous relationship. I knew that more was possible, and I had a big toolbox to create this demand. I had the pleasure of learning from two of the kindest and most conscious facilitators I know on this planet, the Founder of Access Consciousness®, Gary Douglas and his co-creator Dr. Dain Heer. I knew that Honouring, Trust, Allowance, Vulnerability and Gratitude with yourself and with your partner were core ingredients in creating true intimacy and a flourishing, nurturing and rewarding relationship. I was certain that with my experience facilitating people in their work and lives, coupled with the fact that I knew all the tools, I should be capable of doing this relationship differently.

What I actually meant was that I was determined to DO it RIGHT. I am laughing aloud just thinking about it. That point of view made everything much harder than I had foreseen. When you are determined to do something right, it doesn't really give you freedom to create outside your box of judgment. You get stuck in the polarities of right and wrong, which only creates more judgment. And when you are creating from judgment, nothing beautiful really grows.

So, Joakim and I started our journey together with the most nurturing, playful, and alive partnership I had ever experienced. Yet after about a year, we came to a point where, despite our ambitions, we had created something that wasn't rewarding for either of us. My divorce from the children's father had been extremely tough. I had put a lot of energy into guiding the kids and myself through the inferno of emotions, avoiding guilt trips to my best ability. With one foot in the shadow of my past relationship and the other foot in my new one, I ended up creating drama and trauma instead of possibilities. I felt that Joakim had an urge to be needed. He did everything for me, including trying to save me from the emotional upheaval of the divorce. I wanted him to choose for himself, instead of trying to fulfill my unspoken needs. My point of view was that I didn't need anyone. And I definitely did not desire to be saved. In my need NOT to need anyone I also blocked myself from receiving all the gifts that he actually was. I could not receive his love or his caring. Gratitude and allowance turned into judgment, and our relationship became more or less like any other relationship. I made him wrong. I made me wrong. We were supposed to be better than this.

I knew we had to put an end to the insanity and the only way I could do it was by pushing him away, forcing him to break up with me. The minute after creating the break-up, I regretted it. Deeply! However, this choice created a lot of awareness for me, even though it seemed crazy at the time. It was painful in so many ways. For thirty days, I sat down and took a whole new perspective of myself. I looked at every angle of my life, every choice that I had made, consciously or unconsciously, and every fixed point of view that I had, which cumulatively led to the break-up with this kind, caring, gorgeous man whom I still loved and my kids adored.

What was right about this that I didn't get?

I realized that while I had focused on DOING the relationship differently, I hadn't been totally willing to BE everything that was actually required.

JOAKIM:

When I started seeing Hanna, I was happy and excited. Finally, someone saw my gifts and appreciated them! For the first time in a relationship, I was acknowledged for being different—for being me. Hanna brought out the best in me. Where I was stuck in old patterns, she helped me look at new possibilities. This created so much ease in my life. For as long as I could remember, I had made myself wrong for being different from other men. The fact that I was OK the way I was, was completely new to me. I had too often adjusted to the woman I was with, a trait which made me quite colourless and created a separation from myself that wasn't really attractive. This woman actually desired that I be ME.

So with this new smorgasbord of ingredients in the relationship, I was amazed and very much in love. I wanted to do everything for Hanna. Our bodies had connected in a way that I had never experienced before: intense and real. I created a beautiful connection with her kids; everything was totally mind-blowing. And easy. We had fun, and I really felt alive. We were full of hope and dreams, and maybe a little too vested in the outcome. After a while, we started to fall back into old patterns of relationship, even though we did not like it....

Since Hanna was going through a lot of emotional pain, I focused on her happiness. Though she hadn't requested, or even wanted me to, I invested all my energy in her. I truly wanted her to need me, and when she didn't, I felt lost. After standing beside her for a year with my heart wide open, without really being received, I started to get angry with HER. In reality, I was angry with me—for losing myself AGAIN, for not making myself my top priority in my life, and for not choosing to heal the emotional wounds from my past.

When Hanna provoked me to break-up with her, I got so angry that I decided that no matter what, we would NOT get together again. This, of course, was a defense that I put up because I was deeply hurt. In a childish way, I wanted her to hurt too. And when I missed her, I judged myself for being weak.

A new beginning

HANNA:

When we met again after a month, everything had shifted. We had destroyed and uncreated our relationship to be able to create it again, this time with more choice—without the point of view that it had to work, or how it should work. We were willing to look at what was going on, rather than what was supposed to be. We were ready to explore the elements of intimacy together...without me as the project leader.

JOAKIM:

I now realize that we had to destroy what had been to allow us to build something different. After all, we knew something else was possible; we just had to take a different path to create it. Our month apart gave me time to heal and reflect upon my behaviour instead of just blaming

Hanna and focusing on what she had done wrong. When we both stopped doing drama, we were able to create a new beginning.

Our secret points of view

HANNA:

Looking back at what led to our "failure," I see several aspects that brought us to the break-up point. Some of those were my secret points of view (which I would never even admit to myself that I had).

> 1: *I had more life-experience than Joakim.*

Hellooo?! I had THREE kids, and I was six years older than him!! Therefore, my opinion and way of doing things were worth more than his. And, therefore, I was right.

> 2: *I had created more in my life, profession-wise (very successful) and asset-wise (like house, furniture and bank account).*

Therefore, my opinion and way of doing things were worth more than his. And, therefore, I was right.

> 3: *I am smarter than he is.*

Therefore, my opinion and way of doing things were worth more than his. And, therefore, I was right.

> 4: *I know more about relationships than he does.*

Just look at the number of classes I had taken! Therefore, my opinion and way of doing things were worth more than his. And, therefore, I was right.

In summary: ***My opinion and way of doing things were always worth more than his. And, therefore, I was right. Period.***

I exaggerate a bit so you get the picture. How could this attitude create anything but judgement of Joakim and separation between us? It made me a superior b-tch energetically. And it was certainly NOT honouring of him or me.

I am now being "50-50" in our relationship. I am superior to Joakim in several areas (and vice versa), but that does not mean that I use superiority against him. We are both equal in our relationship. It doesn't make sense that my opinion should set the rules for how we live and create our life together. When I look at my points of view as neither right or wrong—just as interesting points of view—it creates more freedom and allowance for us individually and as a couple, and brings more fun and ease.

For an "I-know-how-to-handle-everything-myself" person like I used to be (and sometimes still am), it is not always easy to be willing to be wrong. The interesting thing is that when I am willing to lower that barrier, become vulnerable, let go of the need to know it all, and release control of the outcome of everything, it opens me up to connect with Joakim from a space that creates phenomenal intimacy.

Other points of view that I secretly had:

5: I *should be single for at least a year before starting a new relationship.*

6: He *will regret it if he doesn't have kids of his own.*

I judged myself as weak since I wasn't single for at least a year before Joakim came along. And I was afraid that he would wake up one day wanting kids of his own. (I had made it clear that I was done with that chapter of my life). What did these points of view create? They stopped me from being 100% in the relationship. They stopped me from receiving all of the kind, nurturing, healing, sexual life energy that Joakim was willing to gift to me, and that I had longed for my whole life. It also created self-judgement in forms like, *I am not worthy of him; he would be better off with someone younger without kids,* etcetera. This created more separation between us. I knew with my whole body and being that this man was a huge contribution to me, my life, AND my kids' lives. But stubbornly I was not willing to receive him. So I did a push and pull dynamic: I desired him (pulled him towards me) but could not receive him (pushed him away), again and again, like a yo-yo on repeat. How insane was that?

JOAKIM:

I knew I had found a treasure. During the first year, I think one of our biggest challenges was my fear of losing this treasure. I wasn't willing to lose Hanna, which made me do things that weren't really rewarding for either of us. Some of my secret points of view were:

1: *I wanted Hanna to need me. In order to get her to need me, I decided to try to rescue and heal her.*

Hanna made me feel special. If I could rescue her (from whatever she needed to be rescued from), she would appreciate me more. If she needed me, I would be even more special. If she needed me, she would stay. I didn't see that this neediness created nothing but a jail for her— a jail that led her to push me away.

2: *I did not want Hanna to succeed in her career.*

The selfish part of me wanted to keep her for myself. If she were successful, she would meet even more people, including men—men who would, no doubt, find her desirable. She might find them attractive, and I might lose her. Of course, this energy did not nurture trust. Hanna had given me more freedom than I could ever imagine having in a relationship; couldn't I do the same for her? What kind of a man was I? Self-judgment rang the door.

To add to that, the more work she had, the less time she would spend with me. What if she forgot how special I was? It was like I could not believe that I truly was special. I needed Hanna to prove it to myself.

3: *Since she has kids, I need to show how serious I am.*

Early in our relationship, I stopped seeing my friends because I thought that this proved I was willing to be serious and invest my time. If I wanted to see my friends, I made myself wrong for that desire, even if Hanna didn't mind. I felt bad for not seeing my friends; I felt bad because I wanted to see them. No wonder things got crazy.

4: *Since she has kids, she should make all the decisions. I am less important.*

This point of view didn't allow me to be 50-50 with Hanna; it made me inferior to her! Because I never made my needs important and I judged myself as egocentric if I put my needs first, it did a lot of harm to my confidence as a man and a partner. No wonder I felt confused.

Choosing each other every day

HANNA:

Today we are happily married. We don't have an agenda to stay married until death do us apart. We make a choice every day to be together. And as long as we are both contributing to each other we will stay together. We don't have a perfect relationship—but we do have an AMAZING one! It's a relationship that works for US: kind, caring, nurturing and playful most of the time. We don't DO relationship perfectly, but we are willing to BE what is required to make it work, without divorcing from ourselves and without judgement or fixed points of view of how marriage should be done. We are continuously asking questions, looking at what is working and what is not; we are both willing to be wrong, and we have a lot of ease with changing stuff that comes up.

There are still moments when one of us chooses drama— for a minute or two. When that happens, one person just calmly asks, "Are you aware that you are doing drama right now?" without trying to fix it or save the other person from it. This makes the one doing drama realize how silly that choice is, and invites the question, "For what reason would I continue to choose the upset?" Then it is over. After all, the emotional reaction in your brain only lasts for eight seconds. After that, it is your choice to be angry, upset, or whatever. If we have no judgement about our partner having an upset, it gives them more freedom to make a different choice.

Joakim and I create greater possibilities together than we do apart. I am a mover, creating and getting things done at the speed of light. I'm also the mind-tripping one, always rushing into new things. Joakim moves at another pace. He is down-to-earth, extremely present in the now, and has a connection to his body that I secretly envy. When I don't judge what Joakim is NOT and instead have gratitude for what he IS, our relationship gets even greater. I can receive his gifts, and he can receive mine.

JOAKIM:

Hanna is my best friend and a fantastic partner in life. Sometimes we disagree, but we don't judge it as wrong. We are still learning about ourselves and each other; as long as we enjoy growing together, it is easy to choose to be in our relationship. I ask myself regularly, "Is this the relationship that matches the energy of the request I made to the universe," and the answer is still yes!!

I don't think there is a universal recipe for a happy relationship; everyone has to ask questions to see what works for them. Continuously. Every day. What works today may not work tomorrow. What I know from personal experience is that if you divorce yourself in order to be with someone, you are probably off track. Being true to oneself is vital. I think Hanna captured that well in the song she sang to me at our wedding.

You are such a gift being YOU!
How could I not say "I do"?
You are a heaven to touch,
You know you taught me so much
How cool that you did arrive
Together we're gonna thrive.
You're not too good to be true.
I am so glad you are YOU!
It's not so easy to dare,
let go, to choose—not compare.
To create what we know is true,
No matter what others do.
To make a choice every day,
Be greater than yesterday.
I don't know what that will be,
If we keep moving, we'll see.
I love you baby,
And if it's quite all right,
I'll ask you baby
To warm my feet at night.
I love you baby,
Trust in me when I say:
Don't change you baby
No matter what I say,
Don't leave you baby,
You'll always be okay,
If you just follow
what is true for you.

About the Authors
Joakim and Hanna Valdevi

Joakim and Hanna Valdevi live in beautiful Stockholm, Sweden, together with Leon 13, Ossian 9, and Tilia 9. They are both driven entrepreneurs and business owners, and all of their daily work is dedicated to creating a different reality. Hanna works with people's minds, Joakim works with their bodies and together they empower people to grow and prosper.

Hanna has a Master's degree in Business Administration and worked as a manager in International companies for 15 years. She is the owner and co-founder of Excelleragruppen AB, where she works with leadership and management training, team development and business coaching. Hanna is a certified professional coach and leadership trainer, EQ-consultant and is an Access Consciousness Certified Facilitator. She has the ability to get beyond the walls that

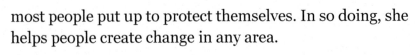

most people put up to protect themselves. In so doing, she helps people create change in any area.

Joakim is a trained Health Educator, Massage Therapist, Personal Trainer and is now in his fourth year at Stockholm College of Osteopathic Medicine to become DO Osteopath. His skills with bodies are asked for worldwide, and he travels the world, facilitating and creating change. He works with people's inner and outer strength, primarily by bypassing people's mind and talking directly to their bodies.

Relationship Unlearned

BETSY MCLOUGHLIN

I wonder, did you have role models teaching you about relationships? Did you learn how to have a generative partnership, and what that requires from both partners? Did anyone talk to you about communication? Or what intimacy is? What about give-and-take? How about compromise and allowance? Or did you have to unlearn everything you saw growing up, like I did? I always thought courses about communication, intimacy with self and others, and creating abundant relationships should be taught in school. These courses would have helped me tremendously; I stumbled around in the dark blindfolded for quite a long time on most of these subjects.

Ladies, did you envision having a knight on a white horse sweep you away in a passion-filled embrace and ride off into the sunset? Did you spend time fantasizing about your wedding day with a beautiful dress and a picture-perfect husband? I sure thought that if only I had a guy who would treat me like a princess, my life would be amazing. Cue "fade screen." And then what? Growing up, I would lose myself in books, devouring the words and yearning for that special someone to be in my life. I never thought past the romantic fantasies that books and movies portray as "relationship."

To say that my parents were not kind to each other is an understatement. They did not have an intimate partnership or speak lovingly as I thought a married couple should. Because my bedroom was right next to theirs, I often overheard their fights with all the ugly things they yelled at each other behind closed doors. The shouting would grow so loud that I would put my hands over my ears and beg silently for them to stop the cruelty. Many nights, I buried my head under the pillow, sobbing, feeling alone and helpless to do anything about it. It didn't stop in the bedroom...they also shouted nasty things at each other in front of my siblings and me. It certainly was not a relationship I had any desire to replicate.

One day when I was seventeen, I was on the phone with a friend making plans to go out when Dad started yelling because there was no butter in the house. Mom had decided to buy only margarine, and this tipped the scales. His yelling and anger escalated quickly to the point where he hit Mom firmly in the middle of her back. She doubled over in pain and screamed. I think the wind was knocked out of her for a couple of moments. Absolutely devastated, I quickly got off the phone and made plans to get out of the house that night. I tried to forget what happened as best I could, but I had just witnessed what I had suspected for years—Mom's bruises were not the result of her clumsiness or her running into things. She always explained them away, and I chose to believe her. Before that incident, it was too difficult to acknowledge what I knew deep down, so I swallowed the lies. I had learned how to bury the truth and become an expert in denial.

I recently realized that I had blamed my parents for not teaching me how to have a relationship. Somewhere, I thought I had no idea how to create a successful relationship on my own since my parents were so messed up. Even that decision is quite mired in mud. Wow! I'm so grateful for that awareness. What lessons did I learn so I could choose way beyond their marriage and create what works for me? What questions can I ask from what I grew up with? What judgments can I release of my parents and of myself?

Being Adopted

I have always known I was adopted; I am grateful my adoptive parents told me the truth about my history instead of finding out later on in life. My birth mother never informed my birth father or her parents that I existed. She turned me over to the California Children's Home when I was a few days old. After being adopted by a wealthy family (family #2), I was with them for only a couple of months before the head of the household discovered he had a terminal illness, at which point they decided they could not raise me. Family #2 took me back to the Children's Home where a foster mother (family #3) cared for me until the couple who became my "permanent" parents (family #4) adopted me at six months old. All of this was slightly confusing for a child to wrap her head around. Am I confusing you telling the story? Haha!

Hearing this story as a young girl, I decided at some point that I was unlovable and that no one wanted me; everyone abandoned me and always would. After all, I had four different families by the age of six months. This conclusion was the basis for a great amount of turmoil and angst in my life. How do you NOT have any type of relationship with the person who gave birth to you? It shaped my self image, and made me feel like I was less valuable than other people.

Have you ever noticed that what you decide becomes a self-fulfilling prophecy? I decided that no one truly loved me and cemented that belief into place. How did I do that? I created friendships and relationships with impossible standards. If I didn't feel I was lovable and didn't love and honor myself, how could anyone else possibly do that for me? Talk about setting myself up for failure and disappointment.

I fell in love in college, and the early stages of being together were blissful for several years. Our physical and emotional connection was everything I had dreamed of. We married when I had barely turned 20. Though I was happy to start my own household and leave the toxic environment of childhood behind, I had no clue how to create a loving home. I also had not equipped myself with any tools for creating a happy life for myself.

At the time I met my husband, I was a nationally-ranked tennis player. I loved traveling and competing, and I truly enjoyed teaching people the joys of tennis. I could make the ball go anywhere I intended most of the time, and it was magical. All my problems disappeared when I was on the tennis court, and I felt free. My body enjoyed playing too; with the sun on my shoulders I felt powerful, potent and sexy. I loved the tennis life, yet I chose not to pursue becoming a professional on the international circuit because I wanted to have a "normal" life with my husband. I became burned out from intensive training and chose to take a break.

Hubby told me he didn't want me around a lot of men wearing what he deemed "skimpy" tennis outfits. I completely agreed to his requirements. In an effort to please him, I turned my back on my life in tennis and chose to work in office environments. Little by little, I lost more of myself in these temporary jobs that I did not enjoy. I missed the joy that tennis gave me. I missed my friends and working out. I yearned for the joy of playing and having time for me but I didn't say anything. This led to bitterness and resentment towards him and toward myself. I became angry at me for not voicing what I required to be happy. Mom had taught me that "you keep your mouth shut and do what your husband wants," damn the consequences. And I was the "dutiful" wife (whatever that meant to me). I was so confused and muddled about what I thought was the right thing to do as a wife vs. what I wanted. I buried all these feelings deep inside and did my best to soldier on.

Within a couple of years, I was completely miserable and developed several illnesses. I was not kind to my husband or to myself. Mimicking my mother's behavior, I yelled at him and manipulated him with passive-aggressive nagging. I had no grace or gratitude towards him and told him all the time what a terrible husband he was. In turn, he vacillated between totally ignoring me and being verbally abusive. We lobbed bombs back and forth with increasing intensity and devastation. As time went on, our relationship (or lack thereof) and my self-esteem deteriorated so much that I started considering suicide. I didn't tell anyone how unhappy I was. Instead, I put on a happy face while at work or with family. I was a master of disguise, as I had been growing up. I left my phone disconnected most of the time, avoided friends and social activities, and disappeared as much as possible. I didn't know where to turn or who to ask for help as I sunk deeper and deeper into the black hole of depression.

After six years of treating each other with disdain in this increasingly toxic relationship, our marriage finally dissolved. Even though I would shout at him that he should just leave, I was still surprised when he actually chose to end our marriage. After all, our vows were for "better or worse" and until "death do us part."

For a long time, I blamed Hubby for everything wrong in my life. I blasted him for leaving me and for not being willing to go to counseling to try to save our marriage. I thought I hated him for the fact that I had to take another job that made me miserable just to have a steady income. I didn't look at where I might have imploded the demise of our marriage, which was certainly not very kind to either of us! It was much easier to look at everything he was doing wrong instead of examining my own contributions.

Continuing the Drama

My second marriage repeated a similar pattern of unhappiness for many years, until the day I said "STOP." What in the world was I doing? Here I was, creating the same thing AGAIN. We were both unhappy but had no idea how to change it.

Fortunately for myself and our relationship—I chose to change my behavior. I realized that I was replicating my parent's abusive partnership and that it WAS possible to choose something different. Hubby was willing to shine the light on the dark areas of our relationship that we had neglected and ignored.

We went to counseling—individual and couples. This helped me become clear about everything that wasn't working for me or for us. Honestly, for quite a while we didn't know if we would stay together or not. I finally realized that I could only change ME. I could not change Hubby, no matter how HARD I tried. I started to realize how much I had been choking the life out of our marriage by trying to control everything and everyone. No wonder I felt like I was suffocating and wanted OUT. Ouch! I can only imagine that he was feeling a lot of the same things. He has told me that it was so easy to blame me for all the problems we were having without taking responsibility for his part in our personal telenovela.

I shifted the intensity of my criticism and control from blaming Hubby to regaining myself. Somewhere I had bought the point of view that if I could control everything and everyone, everything would go the way I demanded. Can you guess how well that was working? Everyone loves to be told what to do all the time, right? Yikes! Does criticizing and controlling ever create a nurturing environment? As I constricted and micromanaged more and more, I suffocated the possibilities out of my relationships—at home, at work, and in all other areas of my life.

I began to look at all the places I had been hiding and cutting off pieces of myself to please everyone—everyone EXCEPT me. I had lost myself and somewhere decided that *I* did not matter. I used to be fun, loving, and vibrant and had somehow replaced that person with a depressed, nagging, sick recluse. I was willing to look at the not-so-pretty parts of myself and what I had created in order to release the guilt about what a horrible person I had become.

I recognized that in order to change my life, I had to let go of the point of view that I was the worst wife and mother ever. What if what I had done wasn't awful or wonderful? What if it was simply the choice I made at that moment in time? When I was finally willing to give up justifying the rightness of my choices, and beating myself up for the stupid ones, I realized that I could finally have freedom in choosing for my future. So, guess what? No matter what you've chosen in the past, YOU can choose something different now, too! If that isn't working, choose something else! What if there is nothing wrong or right with what you've done in your life either?

What if we changed the paradigm around our relation-ships? What if we nurtured and fertilized ALL our relationships and RELEASED the need to micromanage everything around business, friendships, partnerships, and our significant other?

Do you give your partner space to contribute to your relationship? What if you didn't make anyone wrong (even you)? What if your partner doesn't respond in any of the ways you expect? Would you be willing to let go of your expectations of what partnership should or shouldn't look like?

I crawled out of the hole of illness and depression by choosing for me instead of against me. I began choosing life, happiness, and most importantly—ME! It was time to have a deep friendship and communion with myself. Fast forward a few more years and the relationship I have with my husband and myself is now completely different. In fact, all my relationships are different. They are real; there is no more pretense. I am silly, playful, and willing to make mistakes. I don't take myself so seriously, and I am willing to be vulnerable. I'm willing to have people see the real me—not someone I thought people wanted to see. I am creating amazing friendships and have friends all over the world who contribute to me, and I contribute to them creating magical possibilities. I am truly blessed and grateful.

Friendship With Me

I spent most of my life ignoring myself and choosing to only exist. I allowed many aspects of life to pass me by. My relationship with ME continues to evolve and improve because of my willingness to ask for more. I am not nearly as unkind to myself as I used to be. Do I have moments of judgment or slip into old behavior patterns? Yes I do. These moments have become further and further apart. When I realize I'm doing it, I simply STOP. I giggle at myself for the choice I made in those minutes of unconscious behavior and say, "Thank goodness I know how to change this uncomfortableness FAST!"

I understand the power of asking questions without having answers. This is completely opposite from how I functioned for most of my life—I thought I was successful if I knew the answers. I was an excellent problem solver. I thought I enjoyed figuring things out. What if this was all a distraction? I've gladly resigned my problem solver role.

I began asking questions that I learned from my magical friends Gary Douglas and Dr. Dain Heer. "What else is possible that I haven't ever considered?" and "Who am I today and what grand and glorious adventures can I have?" are two examples of questions that have created amazing results. I have asked countless questions and attended many classes to create the changes I demanded for my life.

I got over the point of view I had about *another* failed marriage and became willing to lose my marriage that was on the brink of extinction. In being willing to lose everything I thought I had to have, we were finally able to create the marriage I desired but didn't really believe I could actually actualize. Before this amazing journey, I did not know it was possible to have such a shift!

I longed for trust, allowance, gratitude, and true partnership; qualities I had looked to everyone else to give to me. When I recognized that controlling and micromanaging don't work, I finally saw I had snuffed out the possibility of growth, change, and fun! Phew—so grateful for that awareness.

My husband and I talk and laugh all the time. Do I slip into moments of control? Yes, I do. And when I realize I'm doing it, I change it by laughing or exaggerating the behavior to ridiculousness, which lightens the mood quickly for both of us. Hubby might even join in the exaggerated silliness, which contributes to more laughter. That's such a change from the days where I would have been passive aggressive and angry in silence for days on end when he didn't do what I wanted. The nerve—how dare he not be my puppet!

Have you ever been at a restaurant and seen a couple sitting in silence or arguing through dinner? That used to be us—angry and uncomfortable, with no idea how to talk to each other. When I see that now, I am so grateful that we've changed that.

Demanding a life full of adventure with a partner and friends around the globe is more than I ever dreamed possible. And I feel like it's just the beginning. What grand and glorious adventures await me now? What can I contribute to creating greater than yesterday with all my relationships?

I shared with you the drama story I wrote, directed, and starred in to show that you absolutely can change your life! What would you like to create? Is there an area of your life that you have ignored or glossed over? What would change if you were willing to shine the light on what isn't working? What if it's not as difficult as you might envision? Would you be willing to do this without judgment or recriminations? What if everything was simply an interesting point of view? Do you know you have total choice to choose different every moment of your life? I have learned that being in allowance of everything creates so much ease. Everywhere I used to fight, resist and react to things out of my control, I now relax and allow people to choose what works for them— NOT what I think works for me. This space of allowance for choices is freeing—I dare you to give it a shot and see what it might create for your life.

How would you enjoy treating you? Where are you not contributing to yourself—that if you would contribute to you—would change everything?

What if YOU were the kindness to you that you wish others would gift you? I yearned for love and affection from people who were incapable of giving it to me. Do you see how that kept me tied up in a loop of hungering for something and never receiving it? I used to look to others to fill the hole inside of me. When I started filling that hole myself, I gained confidence, and now I trust and like myself! I know I have my own back and that I'm a strong, vibrant, capable woman who can do anything. I've only just begun, and there are many more adventures and friendships awaiting.

How much more can you be for others when you are present in your life—for you? Would your relationships flourish if you fertilized them? How many blooms can you witness? It's an absolutely beautiful thing to see the blossoms opening up for all to enjoy.

Are you ready to be nurturing to you? Are you writing the adventure of your life including the messes, mistakes, miracles, giggles and play?

Let's embrace the joy of living!

About the Author
Betsy McLoughlin

Betsy McLoughlin is an International Best-Selling Author (this marks Betsy's eighth book), a Radio Show Host and a Certified Facilitator. She is a transformational coach, a Body Process Facilitator, and so much more! Her vibrant personality is the space of no judgment and is the catalyst for quicker success and happiness for her clients.

This creator of magnitude has inspired hundreds and has been featured on The *Ask BonBon TV Show*, numerous radio shows and tele-summits. The radio show Betsy co-hosts with beautiful Kathy Williams, *Imperfect Brilliance* can be found on iTunes Podcast or on YouTube.

Betsy is also a magical Realtor® who creates ease for her clients. Her calm demeanor, willingness to ask questions outside the box and look for what else is possible creates more opportunities for her clients.

Betsy would love to create new possibilities with you. Are you ready? Check out her websites at www.creatingyumminess.com and www.imperfectbrilliance.com and find her on Facebook. She has a special offer for you - a free, 30 minute session to explore your world. Email her at accessbetsy@gmail.com.

Old Maid Be Damned!

By Christine McIver

How is it possible that after all this time I still don't have the love of my life? It wasn't supposed to be like this. The plan was to grow up, find a man, fall madly in love, and live happily ever after. Damn it! I will die the saddest person in the world if this doesn't happen. What is wrong with me, that I'm over 40 and still haven't figured this out?

My life had been laid out for me. As the ninth of ten children I watched my older siblings around me fall in love, get married and begin to have babies right away. They were so happy; their children brought forth so much joy and laughter. Like many families, we had a lot of dysfunction, and the babies were a major bright spot in the middle of it all. I knew this was what I, too, would have...or so I thought.

By the age of 20, I was sure I was doomed because I still had not found a man and gotten him to propose to me. My brothers would tease me that I was too ugly to have a man choose me, and older folks would often say, "Where is your boyfriend? It's your turn next." TICK TOCK, TICK TOCK. It seemed to me that the pressure was everywhere. My mother would often refer to single women as "Old Maids," and I shuttered at the thought that people would call me that. It was considered a very negative title, one I would do anything to avoid. This consumed my every thought.

I grew up in a very rural community where everyone knew everyone else's business. I couldn't escape the truth that my friends were all getting married, and I was still alone. "THAT'S IT!" I exclaimed to myself, "I am going to find a man no matter what it takes."

No different from a hunter grabbing his gun and setting out for the woods to capture his prey, I dressed for the part, with my weapons of choice: short skirt, sexy top, high heels, lips and eyes sparkling. I scouted out the next event where men would be plentiful, and the game was on.

He was cute, dark hair, dancing blue eyes, great smile, and what a charmer! PLUS, he was flirting with me. ME! That was it, SUCCESS. I wouldn't be an old maid after all!

It was October 1983, and I had finally found my man. Now, on to making it work. We began dating, met each other's families, and as a great bonus, we were both Irish and Catholic. Fantastic! It had to mean something special. Everything was falling into place. We had sex, and it was good. Within the first year of meeting, we had moved in together, gone on vacation, and bought a house. Yes, it wasn't in the usual order or that of all the other girls, but it was still real. He would propose soon—I was sure.

We finally got engaged with a lot of pushing on my part. I wasn't going to go backwards. What would they say about me then? Our first wedding date was postponed because we needed to work on our relationship. No sooner had we decided to postpone the wedding, we found out I was pregnant. The baby had not been planned or manipulated by me, as some later suggested. But now we HAD to get married. I was so excited, doing everything I could to avoid the fact that he was ignoring me; not holding down a job; drinking more than most; and that the arguments were intense—beyond the average for a young couple.

The big day finally arrived, the one I had been targeting since I could remember. February in Canada could be risky with snowstorms, icy roads, and hydro outages. Instead, we had dense fog, a flooded basement, and no hot water. But the real storm ensued the moment my mother saw me in my wedding gown. The first thing out of her mouth was, "Are you pregnant?" *Shit!* I ignored her. *I have to make this work even if she's mad.* Walking down the aisle, she leaned in and whispered to me, "It's not too late." Wow! My mother, the good Catholic woman…never in my wildest dreams would I have thought she would support me walking out of a church full of her relatives, pregnant and single nonetheless. Nope, I was going through with this. After everything I had done to finally get here—this was my dream!

Looking back, that day was a comedy of errors, with more signs of STOP from the Universe than you could imagine. By the end of that roller coaster day, I was emotionally ripped apart, screaming that this was the WORST day of my life, as my newly-engaged brother and his fiancé drove us to our honeymoon suite for the night.

The marriage lasted thirteen months and three days, ending only after my husband chose to strike me. I am so grateful he did. It was the wake-up call I required to see the truth. Oh, I blamed him totally and completely: he did this; he didn't do that; how could he do this to me? It was madness! (Is that what they mean by falling "madly" in love?)

I left the shattered relationship and began my life as a single mother with my 6-month old son in my arms, along with some used furniture, a bunch of debt, and a very bruised ego. It was a massive struggle. Now I was solely responsible for this beautiful boy; I had to continue. Within a year and a half, my now ex-husband had moved miles away and would have nothing to do with raising our son. As for me, I returned to college, gained more self-confidence and secured a job that was something I was finally proud of. Only then was I able to again entertain the idea of finding a man.

Five years had passed, and I was different now. Or so I thought. It was 1990, and we had stepped into the world of telephone dating. What a different world! My next significant other and I would talk for hours and hours on the phone, raking up a small fortune in long distance charges. We discussed every topic imaginable. I was sure THIS one was going to be different. After a month of getting to know each other, we met in person. He didn't look anything like my ex and lived in another city, so he didn't know anything about my foolish past. As it would turn out, this relationship had many of the same issues as the first, with one very significant addition: my increased determination not to fail. I asked no questions about what was possible, or about what was true this time, with this person. I had simply made the firm decision that I would not fail again. What would it say to the world if I failed a second time? Besides, now that I had a child, I was lucky that any man even wanted me. He had a home, a good job, and he even had a washer and dryer. I know how crazy that sounds, but I had waited for so long to have these things that it made this relationship even more important. He also liked my son, and because my ex wasn't in the picture, this was like a cherry on top. I should count my blessings and be grateful for another chance at love, even with a child.

This insanity kept me in the relationship for nine years. Despite the fact that I left and returned more than five times, I was fixated on making it succeed. We did things different yet again. We got pregnant, had a beautiful baby girl, and then got married. One week after we said our "I do's," the entire fantasy came crashing down. We had created so much anger and sadness that the fairy tale could no longer contain the lies. It was clearly an abusive relationship on both our parts. This nearly did me in. I nearly did me in. A dear friend once told me, "Christine, a relationship should build you up, not bring you down." These words grew louder and louder, especially after crying for hours, imagining how I would end it all for him and then me. Now I knew I had to get out of the prison I had created. To hell with what anyone would say or think. I would create a new dream, and I would have joy for myself and my two children. My mental state was at severe risk of going to crazy town with no return ticket. Yet thankfully through it all, there was that whisper that wouldn't go away...*You deserve better*!

And so for probably the 15th time, I left for the final time. Many doubted that I would get out of this crazy loop, but I knew that this time would definitely be different. You see, my son was now at risk on a deep emotional level. He was becoming scared and depressed, withdrawing into himself and showing signs of detaching from his true joyful self. I could put up with a lot but it was by looking at him and really seeing what was happening that motivated me to finally change it.

If I thought being a single mother the first time was a struggle, this time it was a nightmare. My teenage boy and toddler were both reeling from the breakup. My ex refused to have anything to do with my son, as it might cost him child support, all the while doing all he could to turn my daughter against me. Every day seemed to have more problems, more bills, and more sadness. How would I ever get out of this? How would I ever be happy? What did I do wrong? Why can't I get this right? The old self-judgement was on full throttle now 24/7. I stayed in the rabbit hole of wrongness for about six months. Then the determination rose up in me, but this time, it flipped. Instead of desiring a man, I went in the opposite direction. "To hell with men. I am going to climb the corporate ladder, make a success of myself and have the home that we all deserve." So began a 14-year journey of cutting men out of my life, out of my bed, and out of my heart. Never again was I going to have a man hurt me. I didn't need a man. I could do it all myself. The pain I had paid for my desires was too high.

If only I could get the old dream to die as well.

New targets had been set, and I knew I could succeed. I would go back to school, upgrade my education, get a great job in the Human Resources field, and become involved in the local HR community. Check, check, check. My career became my lover. I gave it all my energy, and I nurtured it so it would never leave or betray my love. The results of my efforts were tangible, and I was becoming well known in my field. Now the Director of HR for an international organization, I built my own home and was making six figures. From the outside, I was a success! People were praising me, my strength, and independence. I had created all this, yet my kids were continuing to struggle and I was still very lonely and incredibly angry.

The ever present ache in my heart was starting to awaken again as if from a long winter's nap. If you pretend that something is okay long enough, you begin to believe it yourself. Until you can't anymore. Like a whiny child, my "must happen or else" fantasy was making its presence known again.

While many things had been missing in my past relationships, different things were missing from my new lover: career. Career didn't laugh with me; didn't share a meal or a nice glass of wine; didn't hold my hand or put its arms around me. My career couldn't smile at me and show me a kind word or caressing touch. I became more and more frustrated, agitated and resentful. I was investing so much time and energy, yet at the end of the day there still seemed to be something missing. The emptiness I felt from the absence of a relationship was taking up more real-estate in my days than I could handle.

The time had come. I absolutely had to look at this before the level of sadness grew into massive self-judgement and full-blown depression. How could this be different? Was it possible that it could turn out better than I ever imagined?

During this awakening, I came to a point at which my HR career wasn't enough anymore. What was once exciting, fulfilling and a platform to assist others in creating more joy had become an arduous, exhausting, paperwork-drowning office cop role that sucked the life out of each day. The pressure took its toll on me mentally. It was time for a significant change. That change only came after an emotional breakdown, during which I hid myself away for six months, lost in darkness, behind closed curtains and unanswered phone calls. Confused and skittish, I didn't know how to move out of it. My old boss and friend called me and demanded that I walk every day until I thought I could walk no more and then keep going another 30 minutes. He too had experienced this level of emptiness and was willing to push me until I was out of my hole. I'm so grateful he did!

Once I started to emerge into the light, I looked at what I really loved to do. A short time later I took my skills and talents and started my own coaching and consulting business. I always knew more was possible and with this knowing I started to create what turned me on and lit me up.

It was at this time that the following awareness became my new acknowledgment:

It is not someone else's responsibility to fill my joy bucket.

When you are ready to move forward beyond where you have always operated it can be scary; it certainly was for me! There is no roadmap. Your brain searches and searches, trying to pull you back into the entrenched path you have walked so diligently. What if there could be another way? I started to step into more questions in order to create new possibilities. How will this work? What shall I choose? What do I really desire? Who am I?

In my search for all of those answers, I became aware that I had to become the bridge. Discovering more of me would bring me to the places of joy that I so deeply yearned for.

To move from the lies of "less-than" to the truth of me, I became the bridge. I connected with who I am and what is true for me, not from a place of "should" but from a place of desire, without making any of my desires wrong. It has been essential for me that I move beyond seeing men as the enemy and being at the effect of any of my past choices. I no longer make myself wrong for any choice I have ever made, and I don't make past partners wrong for what they have chosen. This has allowed me to be present with myself and to be present with everyone, whether they are my lover, a friend, a client, or a stranger I meet.

I am happy to say that I have started choosing relationships again, no longer choosing to make them bad or something to avoid. I know now that if you desire more opportunities in relationship and are open to all ways of meeting people— whether that be online dating, hiring a professional dating service or going to events—by doing what works for you, possibilities multiply. My suggestion is: don't believe you have to do it a certain way. When we do that, we cut off receiving—receiving joy, pleasure, friendship, and more from anyone or anything. Remember to honour you; you could choose to have a lover no one knows about, or a boyfriend your family never meets! Experiment to find more of you if that interests you.

You can have the kindness and nurturing of a partner without you or anyone judging the way it shows up. If you are willing to enjoy yourself without the judgement of right and wrong, you will continually open to more in your life.

Ask, "What would I like to have in a relationship?" One of the things I love the most is when someone creates space for me and with me. Leaving the judgements behind of myself, my past, my body, and my life allows that to be created now with so much ease and joy.

The story is not over. I'm not sure where it goes, but I am extremely grateful for every choice I have made. Each has led me to the person I am today. No choice is a wrong choice. Every choice has led to an awareness of what I enjoy (or don't!) What would change for you if you were to visit each of your past choices and examine them to see if they carry judgement, regret, or shame? If they carry any of those, see where you are willing to have more allowance and gratitude for them and what they created for you. The past can haunt us, but we can change it if we are willing to be vulnerable with all of it. It is your life! It is your joy. No matter what, choose for YOU!

About the Author
Christine McIver

Christine McIver, TV & Radio Personality, Speaker, Possibilities Coach, and Potent Creator of Magnitude and Access Consciousness Certified Facilitator®, is driven to inspire you to make choices that will bring you to your true heart's desires.

Christine lives her life out loud and is a natural cheerleader who believes in the abilities of others to change their lives quickly and easily. She entices clients to show up more in their life, business & relationships than they have ever before, inviting them to make all that they once knew was possible, possible.

Throughout the many choices she has made in her own life, Christine knows today that all of those choices, good, bad or otherwise, now serve her and her audience.

Programs with Christine include Divorce with Dignity, Beyond the B.S. Business Studies, Be The Dominatrix of YOUR Life, and personal VIP coaching for individuals and entrepreneurs.

Christine is also an Access Consciousness Bars®, Body, Facelift Facilitator and Right Body For You® Taster Facilitator.

Christine has impacted thousands of individuals both in Canada and abroad with her enthusiastic message of possibilities. Her kind, direct and joy-filled approach is both comforting and stretching. Christine believes that all things are possible beyond what is present in anyone's life, business or relationships.

You can find Christine the following ways:

Christine@inspiredchoices.ca

www.inspiredchoices.ca

www.inspiredchoicesnetwork.com

Creating Your Symphony

By Cassy Summers

If you are reading my chapter, I suspect you are a curious seeker. Perhaps the traditional ways of living on this planet don't really work for you. I wonder what magnificent possibilities, beyond anything you have ever seen, are you actually aware of?

Here is my story about the lie of relationship, the journey beyond stability, and how you have the capacity to create a dynamic relationship using energy and questions. I cannot give you all of the how to's in this short chapter, but what I can do is invite you to the energy and the awareness of infinite possibilities. If you can perceive it, you can ask for it and then you are 90% there. I invite you to tap into these possibilities, to know what you know, and make your demand: " No matter what it takes I am having all that I know is possible in this life." Then follow the lightness— the clues of the universe will show you.

~ Foundationless ~

Throughout my life, I have considered myself a romantic, an abundant lover, and a caring partner. I had a great desire to prove my love to the significant people in my life. My secret hopes were that if I could show them enough kindness, love, and gratitude, they would finally be able to stop judging themselves and find a deeper sense of self-value.

I never did succeed.

I believed that to be a good partner you had to learn everything about the other person, then categorize, memorize, and secure this information into a list of needs. My responsibility would then be to check off every single need I possibly could, (usually before the other even knew they had it—bonus points!) so our relationship could flourish. These needs served as a foundation for my relationship—a solid, stable cement beneath our love on which we could build everything, knowing that no matter what, nothing could move us. I did this without even realizing I was doing it; I just thought it was caring. I had bought so dynamically that creating my life around my partner and their needs was how I would be the greatest gift to them, and that doing this would provide us with a sense of security and stability—all crucial for a successful relationship.

Do you notice any of this in you or your relationships? Do you make it your job to meet your partner's needs?

I functioned this way in every relationship; the people I would draw in were attracted to this dynamic. I was always trying so hard to get everything right, which created even greater heaviness in my world as I disappeared more and more. This would lead to me tightening around the foundation of needs and stability, holding to it as though it was the only thing keeping me afloat and the only thing holding the relationship together because I was failing.

What if it was the opposite?

What if the foundation was actually sinking the relationship?

This type of "loving" was wearing and often confused me, as somewhere deep down I had the awareness that there was another possibility. Every time that possibility didn't show up, I grew more hopeless. I was doing everything right; why wasn't it working?

In my hopelessness, I felt pulled to seek something different and began to take notice of the people in the world who were bursting with life, exuberance, and joy. The way they lived didn't match the energy of someone functioning from a stable foundation. The way they were living matched what I still secretly knew was possible, but had lost hope in. I wondered why I didn't see that exuberance in my relationships.

I then began to look at my experiences. Have you noticed that the beginning of a relationship can be sooo exciting, with constant curiosity, delights, and desires? It seems to contain no foundation and little stability, yet constant creation. Imagine having that everyday! Would life be different? Somewhere along the way I had decided this was an impossibility.... But, if it were possible to have a foundationless relationship, how would that work? What would provoke a state of continuous creation?

To me, creation is the energy of living; it is generative, healing and expansive. What would it be like to live with a sense of creation flowing in every area of your life? Look at the energy of a partnership that is always on the creative edge. The couples are ever-changing and supporting each other in that change; they seem to be on an adventure with each other rather than securing a life together. But how can a partnership flourish without stability? We are told that stability is the key to success. Do you see that really working for many people?

The more questions I began to ask, the more I realized that my artificial foundation couldn't support me; it could only support the judgments that I had bought as real. This awareness began to stir the "little bit of me" that still existed beneath the person I had believed I was supposed to be. Hidden somewhere, I was still holding fast to a little grain of sand, an awareness of possibility that I had told myself was just a "fantasy." I waited quietly.

~ Standing Up ~

One day something changed. Or a million things all changed at once, and my awareness exploded! If I could bottle it and give it to you, I would, but the easiest way to describe it is that I stood up. I just stood up and looked at my life. I looked at my grain of sand and chose to let go of an 11-year relationship that included five years of marriage.

I chose me. I chose the "fantasy." Not a fantasy where I went into another relationship thinking that this time it would be different.... My choice was, *no matter what, I'm going to have all of me and all the possibilities I perceive in every relationship, including the one I have with myself.*

Through my seeking, I discovered Access Consciousness®, which offers life-changing techniques, tools, and processes designed to empower you to create the life you truly desire. Through learning the Access tools, I came across a definition of intimacy that includes these elements: honor, trust, allowance, vulnerability, and gratitude. Imagine what it would be like to have real and total intimacy with YOU! I started creating an intimate relationship with myself and began asking even more questions.

If I was finished contorting myself to fit a relationship model that really didn't work for me, what possibilities with relationship could I create or discover that would match the ever-changing, inconsistent me? And what kind of relationship would expand the life I am creating?

~ The Energy ~

I began to look at each relationship around me as though it were a large, complex symphony with multiple energetic rhythms and notes within it. When I would perceive something that resonated with my desires, I would find that beautiful note, for example, "the hum of playfulness," and invite it to show up more in my life—in all ways, not exclusive to romantic endeavors. This enabled me to play with those energies and discover which ones truly contributed to me, to create melodies that made my world sing. I would then take those that expanded and enriched my life and invite more and more of them to show up.

All of these energies began creating something....

The foundation of everything I had decided was real began crumbling away. In its place, more ease, joy, and creative capacities began to blossom. I discovered I could create a vibrant platform that would support my life rather than stabilize and solidify it. It could move with me and would never anchor me down; it would just give me something off which to catapult my creations. What if YOU, being you, are the energy of the platform of no-solidity from which you can create your life? Would you be willing to explore what you know?

I allowed the tools of Access Consciousness to contribute to every aspect of my life. I began functioning from question, choice, and possibility, which has allowed me to know more than I had ever believed I could.

~ Creationship ~

What if you could co-create with your partner (or partner to come) an energy, a symphony for your relationship that would develop its own consciousness? This may sound bizarre, but if there is lightness in this for you, I invite you to drop the cognitive chatter of impossibility and play for a minute.... Everything is energy, EVERYTHING. Your home, your city, even YOU are made of energy. Have you ever had a delightful plant, an aged wooden desk, or even a beloved car that seemed to have its own personality? What if everything has consciousness?

Just as we can create life forms in books, songs, and paintings, we can create such life in business and relationships. The beauty of creating it is that you no longer have to take what life throws at you, wait and see what happens, or settle ever again; you get to create what you would like to have and then it can show up. If along the way you discover something greater is possible than what is showing up for you, you can always ask more questions, and choose and create again. This is a miracle of having no foundation for you and your creations, there in nothing solid and unchangeable. Does this sound like way more fun?

Would it be nice to have a playmate instead of a partner? A co-creation instead of a marriage? Every word has an energy. Would you take a moment to explore these words: marriage, partner, significant other, fiance, playmate, co-creation, enjoyable other? Which words create a sense of lightness for you? What is true for you will always have a sense of lightness to it. Now look at the words that have a heavier energy; the heaviness means there is something untrue in it—there is a lie attached.

I wonder what word would truly describe what you desire to create with someone? Something creative, light, and full of possibility?

What if today could be the start of a totally different reality in regard to this thing we call relationship, whether that is with someone new or with the person you are currently with? When I made the demand that my friends and lovers not judge me, I really hadn't experienced many relationships where that actually existed, but I was aware of the possibility. It lived in my grain of sand and was more real to me then the limitations I saw in the world around me. That day I stood up, I acknowledged the unbelievable: just because I hadn't seen something yet didn't mean I couldn't have it in my life. I demanded that I would do whatever it took to create and have all of the possibilities,

I knew could be true, if I were to choose and create them. Now the people in my life appreciate me for me, and don't try to shape me into something I'm not! They acknowledge and provoke me to see more and more of the greatness of me. What if there are more possibilities here than we have ever been lead to believe?!

As I play with the various romantic relationships or creationships (insert giggle here) in my life now, I am no longer getting stuck in the heavy solidity I used to think was necessary. By letting go of the need to have form, structure, and a solid foundation, I have been able to sculpt relationships that are eternally malleable and changeable. And maybe not so surprisingly, it has been way more fun for me!

I knew, as I began to energetically craft a relationship, that it would have to be different from anything I have ever had before. In order to honor me and all the possibilities I know are available, it would have to be created from that wondrous place of unbelievable knowing. The person I would choose to create with would have a natural energy that would be both congruent (in harmony with) and cohesive (with qualities that bond well) with me and the relationship I've been asking for. We would already be a match, which is different from two people with potential working at making changes to fit together.

What if you already know, within the first little while of meeting someone, if they are a match to you? Things to notice are: Do you feel more expanded, a greater sense of who you truly are, and have a generative energy when you are with this person? Does your energy increase or decrease when you have spent a large amount of time with them? Do you have a sense of ease and joy when you think of them?

You can ask yourself, "Is this person truly congruent and cohesive with me and the life I am asking for?" Remember that which creates a sense of lightness for you is true, that which creates heaviness is a lie. Please follow your awareness, follow your light.

Would you be willing to play in this game of creationship with me? I wonder if you might just be able to tap into possibilities you may have written off as fantasy too?"

Now, imagine that by just adding this person's energy to your life, it will create a ripple of change and expansion. They do not have to do anything other than be them! When they are creating their life and being that space of joy and non-judgement, it will expand your life, and this is true for them regarding you. This is one of the many possibilities available for couples. It is called "contribution," which is the simultaneity of gifting and receiving.

Does this sound too good to be true? Have you given up on the inconceivable dreams you had when you first began to wonder about having someone in your life? Have you decided that it is impossible to meet someone that so easily matches with you? I had. Would you be willing to look at that and notice what feels heavy to you and throw away the lie, please? What IS light for you? What did YOU know before anyone told you what they had decided was true? What possibilities lie within your grain of sand?

You may already be in a relationship and now going into the wrongness of it. If so, STOP. Now. Please. If your current relationship isn't exactly how you would like it to be, that doesn't mean you "chose wrong" or that your relationship is unchangeable. What if you can create something greater with the person you are already with? What if you just weren't given the tools required to create greater until now? In a moment I will share one of the most dynamic tools I know for changing a relationship...just keep moving, you are almost there. What if that foundation you constructed for your relationship isn't as indestructible as you had hoped? And what if that is a gift?

~ Creative Edge ~

One of the most empowering things I have ever learned is that I can actually create my life and every relationship in it.

Sometimes when I meet someone, it's like a whole universe of possibilities opens up. Have you ever experienced that? For me, it starts with a spark and expands throughout my entire body; my blood pumps a little faster, my light shines a little brighter, and I am dazzled. If I perceive that spark in the other person, my enthusiasm heightens, and I begin playing with the multitude of possibilities. What if this energy didn't have to disappear with time?

What would it be like if you created your relationship anew each day? What would it be like to have your entire body melt when you are in your partner's presence, even after 50 years of being together?

Could creation be the key?

When I speak about creating your relationship, I am referring to a space of total vulnerability and absence of judgment, where you wake up and meet your playmate every day as if for the first time. What if it were possible to change every day? What if assuming they will be the same is an unkindness?

Every night before you go to bed you can energetically destroy and uncreate your relationship. Yes, really! You may be wondering why I would suggest such a thing. Look at the entire course of your relationship with someone (it could even be your mother) and imagine that every fight, every awful look, every moment full of tears or disappointment, was like an array of slivers stuck all over you: on your clothes, in your hair, and all over your skin. You live as though you had let the slivers go, and maybe you have, (or partially so), but mostly we accept the slivers and move on. How many energetic slivers do you have covering you? How many are covering the other person? When you destroy and uncreate your relationship with someone, you energetically allow those slivers, (even the deep buried ones that got under your skin), to release and heal. It would be as though they never happened and you could create from present awareness and desires rather than from the pain of the past.

Get the sense of a stable, comfortable relationship. Now get the sense of a relationship that is in the flow of constant creation. Which lights you up with fire and possibility?

~ Your Relationship Symphony ~

An Exercise To Play With:

At what age did you learn what you were supposed to desire in a relationship? Did a number pop up? Age two? Maybe a little older, age six or seven? Most of us started very young. So, how can you be clear on what YOU would like in a relationship and what you know is possible? What if you played a game with it? Would you start by giving up everything you learned from that age until now about what you were supposed to desire? Energetically allow it all to drift away.

Now expand your awareness beyond your body, your town, even the planet. Expanding outward, bigger and bigger, become the universe, the universe of possibility. Allow all walls of separation to disappear and tap into your space of creation. This may not be a cognitive process; it works differently for everyone, so don't worry about getting it right. What if you would allow yourself a space of play and curiosity with it? Now bring forward the energies of what you know is possible and expansive for you regarding relationship. Many people use the image of those energies coming together in a bubble or energy ball. Be in that space and notice what you notice.

Begin to get a sense of these energies coming together, and from this space ask yourself, "What energies would I truly like to have in my relationship?" You may get a sense of joy or happiness, excitement or nurturing. Whatever energies arise for you, invite all of them to come into your creation. You can bring in as many as you would like; there is no limit here.

When you have them dancing in front of you, pull energy from all over the universe through you into this symphony of energies. Keep going until the energy expands and feels alive! From here send thousands of trickles out all over the world to all of the people who resonate with this energy. You can ask, "Who would be congruent and cohesive with this energy I am aware of?" Trickle out some more. Now pull massive amounts of energy through all of the people and through you, into your relationship symphony. Keep pulling more and more and more! Then send trickles out again. Do this a few times; you will know when you are done. By pulling more energy and sending little trickles back, you will create a magnetic effect so they can find you; the people who resonate will be drawn to you.

Once you have created the energy of the relationship you would like to have, and given it life, it can permeate your existing relationship, or draw in someone who vibrationally matches it. If you already have a partner, you can perform this pull and flow with them. How much fun can that be?!

I wonder what it would create if you did this exercise every day for 30 days?

~ Two Secrets ~

Secret number one is that I have NO need of a romantic relationship. I know it's weird. Most people have bought this "need" as so real and true that they cannot even perceive another possibility. The space of needlessness brings a freedom and choice I never knew I had. Having no need means that I can choose to be with someone when it is light, fun, and contributes to me, and I can also choose to be without a partner when that would be more expansive. I have choice, and I play with that choice constantly. I honour the people I am with, and at the same time, I make sure to honour myself.

Secret number two is that I have been studying and experimenting with possibilities in relationship for a while now. I have tried on a few different possibilities, looked at others and played with the energies as a scientist would. This has led to a big "Aha!" in my awareness of what relationships could be, one that is so big and expansive that words cannot express it all, though I would love to invite you to some of the elements I recognize are possible. Perhaps you have also perceived some of them, and maybe you have written them off as impossible. This is my relationship symphony, and I invite you to have any of this that is light and true for you.

Imagine a person, who when they came into your life, would catapult and exponentialize every possibility for you and all your creations. In turn, you would do the same for them, effortlessly. It would create an energy, and you could allow it to conspire with you and your partner in expanding ease, joy, and glory in every aspect of your life. Yes, I said every aspect, because what if your relationship could exponentialize everything, even the parts unrelated to it? Imagine starting a relationship with someone, and your mother suddenly gets nicer, or you receive more clients, you have more energy, your body feels lighter and rejuvenated. What if you started creating more money, and travel, and all those things that you have always dreamed of? What if? . . .

This energy would continue to be re-created yet constantly expanding. You would have total freedom to do and be what you desire without ever being judged by the other. You would never have to function from accepting the other's "faults" because you wouldn't judge their traits as being wrong or faulted. You would instead celebrate each other's willingness to choose, create, and contribute without a conclusion about what they "should" be choosing. There would be total allowance accompanied by a willingness to be direct and clear in what both of you require to be honoured.

In this relationship, there would be a continuous movement from both partners as the energy of the relationship would create itself anew every day. There would not be a start and stop to the relationship creation, but rather, a flow of various speeds, channels, and possibilities. There would always be a question of what more is possible with this person and with this creation of relationship—never a conclusion. What if both people were willing to hear the whispers of the energy of their relationship? Would you be open to allowing the consciousness of the relationship to assist you and your playmate in knowing if something is required, if something needs to change, if a question is being asked of you?

In this phenomenal creation, the pretense of separation would melt away, and the two people could explore the world knowing that someone, no matter where they are, had their back. They could choose, be, and do anything and never be judged or separated from each other, and never be expected to fulfill the other's needs. Each conspirator of this creation would be the invitation for the other to step into more and more of him/herself and out of their comfort zones when asked.

This is the tip of what I know is possible . . . This is what I keep asking for more and more each day. I have been told that I cannot create this, that it is utopian. And yet I have created it in my life in many ways. That limited point of view cannot stop me anymore, and each day I ask to create even beyond what I already have. Please don't let anyone stop you from creating the unreal, unbelievable possibilities you are aware of. Because I have a little secret to tell you: If it weren't possible, you wouldn't be able to perceive it so clearly.

Once you have the energy of what's true for you regarding the possibilities of relationship, follow the things that match it. You may be inspired to dress up for dinner with your husband, or go to the local market one Saturday; just keep following the little clues, and the lightness will get brighter and brighter the more you listen. Please give yourself time and be kind to you, as you create your symphony. Keep asking for more awareness and tools to show up for you.

When I look at this sweet yet dynamically potent energy, it begins to unfurl like petals.... Layers and layers of other possibilities begin to reveal themselves, so I ask for even more. You can keep asking too.

What if this is the possibility that I hid inside that grain of sand so that no one could damage or take it from me? Is now the time to allow this energy, this possibility, and everything you are aware of to come into this world? To dance upon this planet? I wonder . . .

About the Author
Cassy Summers

Dear Curious You,

What would you like to know about me?

My past, my present, my possible futures? The wonderings of my universe? The magic of my creations? The awakening of me?

In 2012 Access Consciousness® came into my life and gave me the most phenomenal gift I have ever received... **ME**. It woke up the person I had put to **sleep**, the person I had made **wrong for being,** and once awakened I had these **tools** to create ease with all the chaos and suffering I perceived around me.

The information they were sharing and what they were speaking to was everything I had always known was **possible,** but had been told was **impossible.** I remember sitting in my first Foundation class, one of the core classes of Access Consciousness, and thinking **"I knew it!"** And the beautiful thing is, that I truly did know, and I am still discovering and uncovering all that I know, all that I had labeled as impossible.

I immersed myself in the tools, the questions, and everything available through Access Consciousness. I couldn't get enough! I traveled to classes and read everything I could get my hands on. I am a little obsessive like that sometimes (insert wink here) and found myself **expanding and changing at an incredible rate.** The more I received, the more **ease, joy, and glory** I began creating and having.

I began to acknowledge my unique talents, capacities, and way of being with people.

I began to acknowledge my gifts with facilitation.

One definition for "facilitate" is to **"make (an action or process) easy or easier."** This is what I do...what I have always done actually, for everyone around me. When someone is **asking for change,** I create an easier, faster **path** to get there. Stepping into this has turned me on to a more **vibrant** and **generative** way to live.

What could be greater than contributing change and consciousness to the beautiful people in this world, the Curious seekers?

Acknowledging the wonderful uniqueness of me and finally using my gifts has been like opening these **incredible wings** I had **tucked away**. How lucky am I to have this incredible platform to blast off from? If you have seen me at an Access class, you may have witnessed me playing with energy, shifting the molecules, and inviting everyone to play in my Curious Universe.

This is me in total joy.

There is much more to share, and many things I would love to gift to you, but I am aware of the **possibilities created with questions**. So I encourage, maybe even dare you, to ask me whatever questions that are rising and dancing in your world.

In Playful Curiosity,

Cassy Summers

Curiousuniverse.ca

curious.universe.cassy@gmail.com

Choosing Communion in Copulation

MARINA McQUEEN

Up until three years ago, I had no idea that being in communion during copulation was possible, especially for me. I have had a long, painful, and tiring journey of recovery from childhood sexual abuse and trauma, and while I did love the *idea* of sexual communion, I didn't know *how* a deep connection could be created and sustained. I felt so damaged and open to abuse, so inept and clumsy in my expression that having the love I do now might as well have been akin to landing in the rainbow rings of Saturn, so far was it from my daily reality. If this is your concern, please take heart! It is possible to transform your love life if it is something you truly desire. I invite you to read my story . . . maybe even allow it to be an invitation to a new dawn for you and your heart.

Why am I writing this? I've always loved the possibilities sex contains, even during my most torturous times with it. I relish the edge of known possibilities, *la petite mort*, the "dark side," the taboo. I delight in bringing out what is hidden and loving it. I love to invert perversions. I nurture the shadow side of myself like ugly ducklings under my wing. Sharing my story honours all those aspects for me. In making choices to expand consciousness and communion in my life, I choose to be uncomfortable, as I allow myself, ugly ducklings and all, to be seen and known. I am uncomfortable as I consider what you might think about me and my story, and in loving that discomfort, I choose to see my automatic defenses for what they are and to counter-intuitively relax *into* my egoic projected points of view of your reactions and responses to what I write here.

If you have been wondering if it is possible for your love life and relationship trajectory to transform, I am offering my story to you as an invitation to something different. Would you be willing to read without ideas of "should" or "shouldn't," allowing inspiration, delight, astonishment, disturbance, and transformation to rise and fall like waves, without having to push anything away? Would you be willing to be aware of your body's responses in a new way? What is it you desire and require? What is your deepest yearning? Will communion create more of what you are asking for, or less?

What communion is not: A story of separation.

There are plenty of valid reasons to choose unconsciousness in copulation and life, some of which you may have in common with me, or you may have your own. In trying to understand traumas, whatever the acts—abuse/violence/

death/torture/rejection/imprisonment/shame—we may create a judgemental perspective such as, *I asked for it, it's my fault, I don't deserve any better, I must hide my body, it's not safe to be me,* and *all men want to hurt me.* These judgements are painful because they are lies. Lies hurt. That's how I have come to know when I believe something that is not true. You'll know that you're believing a lie when there's no resolution from your painful state. Unconsciousness dwells in trying to prove that a lie is true. For example, the statement "all men want to hurt me" was painful and lingering. It was not true, but for years I tried to make it true so that I would never again be hurt by men.

These are the lies I made true:

I believed that as a toddler, I deserved to be sexually abused; it was my fault and I didn't deserve any better.

I believed that I must hide my body; it got me into trouble with men.

I believed that it was not safe to be me; I couldn't BE me without the threat of unwelcome attention.

At birth, I was separated from my mother and adopted six days later. Then as a toddler—about three years old—I experienced sexual abuse from a family member who died before I was ten years old. For several years, I was angry that he died before I had a chance to kill him, I felt cheated and victimised on so many levels. For me, sexual abuse contains and encompasses all abuse: mental, physical, spiritual, emotional and financial. Living as though the abuse (and the reasons for its occurrence) was true, created a life of abusive relationships where I chose to allow myself to be mistreated, denigrated, belittled, rejected, criticised...

used for someone else's purposes. I enjoyed it in a dark, twisted, mixed-up way, and I continued to choose people who treated me as I treated myself. The lure of degradation and submissiveness was so familiar in its seductiveness that I kept choosing it into my late 30's.

What I didn't realise in my early years was that I am a healer with psychic capacities. I am aware of other people's thoughts, physical pain, and emotions as though they are mine. It was only a year ago that I had the realization that the stuff I had been "trying" to get over all my life—shame, resentment, dark confusion, fury, inertia, intensity of traumatic emotion, and unconsciousness with money and men—didn't even belong to me. It all belonged to the man who abused me. His disgust with himself had become my disgust with myself. His intense guilt, regret, and shame became my intense guilt, regret, and shame. As a toddler, these psychic impressions were woven into my identity, which I used as a barrier to keep myself "safe."

From as early as I can remember, I felt like an outsider—like I didn't belong, no matter how hard I tried or my adoptive mother tried to make it like I did. From metaphysical readings and spiritual sources, it was impressed upon me that I should love, adore, and honour myself. I tried but found it very uncomfortable because I had built my identity around being abused in different forms. I kept myself busy and distracted through worrying about what my lovers, boyfriends, parents, or anyone would judge me for next and then I would plan intricate arguments of how I'd prove them wrong and myself right. I recreated this pattern over and over again. The names and faces of my lovers would change, but I kept having the same relationships. I would metaphorically fling open my doors and welcome a new lover enthusiastically, optimistic that this man would be the one who would see me in all my glory, fall down at my feet (not so metaphorically), and love, adore, rescue, and honour me. Instead, playing out the fantasy, I separated from myself, becoming distorted and splintered in relationships laden with illusions, expectations, and judgements.

Relationship: More Separation

It is my point of view that *relationship* describes an experience of separation rather than communion. Consider the word for a minute. Ree-lay-shun-ship. What do you notice? I sense societal agreements and definitions: relationship means he does this and she does that; if such and such doesn't happen it means that your relationship is doomed, or healthy; if you've fallen in love as a teen, you're *infatuated*; if you fall in love in ten days, you're *gullible*; it has to last for it to be *real*. I wonder who makes these opinions seem like truth?

Relationship and copulation seem to come with an implied how-to guide, a formula, and a process: do this to him; touch her like that; do it for 30 minutes, three times a week. I have read some of those manuals, taken some of those courses, and carried out some of the exercises. Sometimes the methods worked. Now, before taking a course, I ask myself, "Will this create separation or communion?"

My previous sexual relationships often had an element of formula about them. Neither of us knew any different. Or, if we did, we weren't sharing it with each other. When I am following "the formula," I don't or can't ask for something different. If I do ask, it may be from the desire to "perform well" or do it "right," rather than from a space of creating more possibility. This honours neither of us. It feels a bit empty or lonely.

There is angularity to this way of functioning in relationship and copulation. There is tunnel vision: I have a point. There is proof and evidence to be analysed and strategised. There is fear associated with the possibility of loss and gain, and a sense of competition. My body is an object. His body is an object. Her body is an object. The deep, dynamic, creative, and expansive heart to heart connection of Being to Being, is impeded by my mind, my plan, my defences. It hurts. I hide. I seek. I pretend.

Because sexual healing is one of my gifts, sex was sometimes a job for me—although I never got paid for it. As a sexual healer, sex was a place where I would lose myself in service to another, which always seemed to give me a brief sense of relief from the angst and trauma of my life. It was easy for me to nurture others, giving myself and my body to those who seemed to need a lot of looking after. (Of course, I also desired care and nurturing but rarely allowed myself to be so intimate as to receive it.) This made intercourse a confusing and conflicted activity. The more sex I had, the more it appeared that I was loved or needed, yet I sometimes disappeared from my body as soon as I was physically entered. I am not sure where I "went"; I was just not present with the sexual partner or the act. Afterwards, I might not even remember that I'd had sex. If I did remember, I might feel guilty, ashamed, afraid and lonely but also validated and secure because I belonged to someone.

In 2012, I had the realisation that I had mixed up the physical sensations of sexual arousal and fear. Armed with my newfound sexual boundaries generated through healing practices, I cautiously began to date a man who evoked strong sensations in my body—what I considered sexual arousal. For our first few dates, he respected my request not to kiss or touch, but the way he looked at me left me no doubt of his desires. How I enjoyed the power I had! If this was the effect boundaries created, no wonder people used them! What I couldn't see at the time was that by lusting after me so openly, he was not respecting me or my request for taking it slow. It was all brand new to me. I didn't even know what "respecting me" looked or felt like. Then one day, sitting on his sofa watching Wimbledon, we progressed to holding hands and kissing chastely. Initially, the sensations were thrilling, however, he wouldn't stop when I asked him to. As I became more emphatic, he looked angry. In a complete departure from my previous life, I asked him if he was, and he confirmed it. I would never have asked a question like that before; I would have just tried to ameliorate the situation. I knew immediately that what I had thought was sexual arousal in my body was actually an intense arousal of fear: I was in danger!

This information changed everything. In a split second, I saw that my body had continually been showing me my true emotional state, and that I had misinterpreted its message. I saw how aware I had been of the many men who had had strong emotional reactions when I said no or that I needed time and space, all the way back to the first man who had abused my trust. I saw how I had relinquished my power in an attempt to create peace and reassurance that I was safe for *them,* soothing them, while abandoning peace and safety for *me.*

Propelled by an energy that had not been available to me until the moment I saw the truth, I stood up, made a remark about having to "get back," and left. This is also something that I would never have done before. I sped away in my car, my legs shaking as adrenaline pumped through my body. Now I knew that the intense sense of helplessness and "relinquishing my power" that I had equated with romance and desire is actually a signal from my body that this person is not safe to be around.

This acknowledgement created a stream of questions: What if sex is not what I thought it was? What if relationship is not what I thought it was? What if romance is not what I thought it was? What if thinking is not as I thought it was? What if nothing is as I thought it was? And if nothing is what I thought it was, what would happen if I could choose to change my thoughts, opinions, and points of view?

Communion in Bed

- ★ What would it be like if you could come together to have sex in an emotional and energetic space in which you could both "be" with no points of view?

- ★ Imagine the intimacy in openly sharing gifts, offering warmth and playfulness, and inviting a greater expansion of sexy possibilities.

- ★ What would it be like to be in this space where your body is receiving: open and non-resistant; present and relaxed; agendaless; honest?

★ Would you allow an uncontrollable space of pleasure and play, in which you are seen as you are in that moment? And, in allowing yourself to be seen, you are healed.

There is a quality of lightness to this copulation. It allows communion...a space of being together without barriers. Somehow, I knew that sex has the power to be healing, nurturing, generative, creative, relaxing, deep, transformative, joyful, timeless, fun, and transcendent.

When you are in communion with the Being and not just the person, with their energy and not just their body, you become receptive. Receptiveness opens the door to communion. The question, "What else would be fun?" invites your body, the other person, the Universe and any energies that would be a contribution—pleasure, healing, nurturing, and the like—to be present. This question is an energetic request, not a verbal one, that you can ask again and again as you surrender to different possibilities.

You may also like to ask:

Who am I copulating with? The person in front of me? Someone else? Am I remembering the past? What does my body know? Am I lying back or am I receiving? Am I performing a service? Am I performing? What information am I receiving from the other? Am I safe? Am I honouring me? Am I willing to say no? To say yes? To ask for more, or something different? What will it be like to have a body part that doesn't belong to me, inside me? Am I hesitating? What is that? Will I be open to it? Am I experiencing this new moment? Am I seeking familiarity? Am I willing to lose sight of the shore? Am I willing to trust? Who is this body between my legs? This Being? Who else is here? Is s/he remembering someone else? A different time and place? Is s/he honouring him or herself? What else am I aware of? Am I in communion with me? Will I choose me in this moment?

When you choose to be aware of more of yourself, you step into more acknowledgement of both you and the other person. In asking questions with curiosity, I am in communion with me. I allow any fears and resistance to have space, instead of pushing them away and becoming disconnected. In communion with me, I am present to what is arising. I am safe.

Judgement

To be in communion during copulation requires that you choose to be conscious with you, which means that the lies have to die. The fastest way to unconsciousness is to judge yourself—for anything. Many times we make choices that end up creating more pain than pleasure. And, what if you didn't judge yourself for that? We always, always, always get another chance and choice. Judging and shaming ourselves are choices, but they don't solve anything; they create separation and unconsciousness. Do you know where you judge and shame yourself? What does it create in your life? What lies are you believing? What are you trying to make true that isn't?

It's easy to blame others for their actions, and we all have a personal responsibility/ability to respond to what we are creating. Maybe you are waiting for an apology before you let go of resistance or blame? I waited for an apology that was never going to come....He was dead! What happens to our lives while we wait with the burden of resentment on our backs? Are your body and life tense and solidified? Are you free to move? Are you furious? Determined? Fearful? Angry? Sad? Heartbroken? Are you present or in the past? What is that creating? While you are judging the other person, can you be unjudged? What are you thinking about yourself as you level judgements at others? Are you a victim of their actions? Are either of you free?

Choosing Communion in Copulation

To me, consciousness is a space with neutrality of emotion where my cognitive mind does not dominate. There is an expansion of being-ness, which can be blissful and even feel like the spaciousness of "nothing." If you meditate, maybe you know this space. Or you may have touched it when absorbed into an activity that creates an awareness of timelessness, where you "lose" your "self" and all that exists is the communion of the essence of *you* and the essence of the activity. Drawing, painting, writing, massage, dance, playing with animals, or relaxing into nature are activities that allow my thinking self to relax. They (and sex) can be portals to a different state, where barriers disappear and there is a sense of harmony. If I notice I am not present in sex, whether re-experiencing fear or flashback, or in my head thinking about something else, the act of noticing shows me I have just become present—a moment of celebration and vulnerability. I say yes to myself, which allows me to expand even more, to experience healing more deeply, to know myself more lovingly, and to share myself more completely with the Being in communion with me.

So if you are sensing a contraction in your world, in your body, in your connection with others, just be with it. Breathe with it. Allow it to sit beside you...inside you. Say hello to it. This is not the time to push it away. You have chosen it, somewhere, sometime. Ask it, "Are you a lie or are you true?" If you don't get a clear awareness or you are confused, you can expand your energy field as far as you can conceive of and then ten million miles more. Now ask again. Is the contraction even there anymore? Maybe it has just...disappeared? If you can still perceive the contracted energy (which indicates a lie), you can choose to let it go. If it doesn't go, maybe you want to keep it for a while. The important thing is not to push it away, no matter how much you hate it. It helped me to think of what I hate as an ugly duckling; it can't help being ugly, it just is. I adore all ducklings, so now I adore what I hate. It takes practice, of course. Are you prepared to do the work? Are you prepared to love your ugly ducklings? Are you willing to allow them to snuggle up to your breast as you keep them warm?

And then, will you allow them to leave?

Communion in sex is impossible without a partner who is also willing to choose it. I now have someone in my life who is open to me, to himself, and to what we are creating. When I long for deeper exploration in a direction that he does not see the value of, I look for a way to demonstrate the value to him. It can be a delicate dance to show through different mediums, the things I am drawn to without pressuring him or giving him power over my sexual experience. I also ask myself what else I can choose so that I don't feel I am missing out in any way. I take the point of view that our communion is not something to be hurriedly defined through expectations and projections. It's ok not to have exactly what I want when I want it. It's ok to be in a liminal space of "not-quite." It's ok to notice my tendency to control outcomes. It's ok to be closed for a while. It's ok to be unreasonable and inappropriate. We are sharing this space together; playing together and vulnerably and honestly exploring new ways of being together.

In the harmony of my Being and all that is around me (that is simultaneously in me) I let go and allow my awareness to expand beyond my cognitive comprehension. As I am this space of neutrality and relaxation, I am defenseless, as there is no identification of me to defend, prove, or make real. It's what I knew was possible as I gazed into the high clouds in the African sky of my childhood and when I made myself small enough to snuggle up to a bee's furry belly as he rumbled in purple jacaranda flowers, drenching himself in golden pollen. I became the clouds. I became the bee. I see and become colours, shapes, textures, patterns, lights and pictures. I fall, fly, merge, expand, and melt into a space of infinite creativity and Being. Diffused throughout the cosmos, we are present in every molecular moment. Being that presence infuses the invitation to commune with greater possibilities of choice in your life.

I trust that my story has shown you that it is possible to move through and out of the imprisoning cage of familiarity—the pain and trauma of abuse—into a space of communion: openness, trust and awareness with yourself, another and your creation together.

In choosing to embark on such an audacious journey, from known pain into unknown expansion, there is a deep awareness of the extraordinariness of life that just wasn't available to me when I was judging myself as a powerless, broken, worthless victim. If you recognise aspects of yourself in my story and you want to change anything about your life, or you have any doubt that you're able to transform, I wonder what is true about that? I wonder what it would be like for you to be free to fly out of the cage into the big blue sky, becoming even more you with every lie you release? And, if you're already flying free, flying high, what else can you see and choose that is beyond even this?

About the Author
Marina McQueen

Marina McQueen is a magical alchemist of possibilities, continually asking: "What else is possible I've never considered or chosen before?", "What would create more communion?" and "Who else would like to play?" Her willingness to choose and to be undefined and unconstrained by what is "normal," creates an uncomfortable place of choice that she employs to inspire herself and others to go beyond everything! Who would we be if we were willing to go beyond our familiar descriptions of who we believe ourselves to be? What if we are not who we think we are?

Marina welcomes the places and spaces of surrender and chaotic creation in herself and others and dynamically invites you to choose to acknowledge what works for you in her generative and playful programs of transformation.

She adores all and new playmates in adventurous conscious living across the globe and Universe.

Connect with Marina by email:
    mcqueenconsultancy@gmail.com

No Matter What You Have Been Through, Anything is Possible!

BY REID GARCIA CFMW

You may be reading this because you are curious about creating something different with relationships. Maybe you would like to create something different with someone you are with; have a better relationship with yourself; change your perspective on relationships; or have better relationships with everyone and everything, including the earth. Yup, you can have a relationship with the earth too!

The words you are reading are not a means to an end, or a way to come to conclusions or answers about relationships....

I am writing not to give you answers, but to bring an awareness of what YOU desire and what you are able to choose and generate in your life. May this be a contribution towards creating a totally different world with relationships.

You will see that I will ask many questions. They are an invitation to look at what you may not have ever considered before. Be aware of what occurs when you read a question: Are you coming up with an answer that limits you or is it a conclusion? Do you think you should have an answer because others have told you that you should? Would you be willing to be undefined and not expect or have any answers? Would you be willing to see if being undefined creates more for you? There is no right or wrong way here, just as there are no right or wrong relationships.

Relationships are what you make them. You create them— they don't happen to you. In the past, I often chose a partner and made them more important than me and my life. When I gave up myself for the other person, I ended up losing a sense of who I was as a being—especially when one of us left the partnership. At the time, I thought I had to spend more time alone rather than be in a relationship so the painful pattern wouldn't happen again; I believed I had no other choices.

When I was with someone else, I would be aware of the other person's desires and think that I had to act on that awareness to make them happy. I'd make their desires most important and make mine secondary. Even if my partner didn't verbalize what she wanted, I'd find myself trying to give her what I thought she wanted. I constantly catered to the other person, which limited my capacity to be and live to my fullest. It's like I condensed myself and my life into the size of an apple when really I am at least the size of a watermelon!

Reid Garcia, CF MW

Your beliefs influence what shows up in your relationships, and you can generate whatever you'd like. If you believe relationships are about distrust and worry, that's what will show up. If you believe they are about joy and fun, that's what you will create.

Perhaps you were not shown that you can have your own point of view about relationships or even about anything in your life. You may have seen your friends, family, and others model certain relationship characteristics or habits and believed that was how you should act too. Growing up, I saw many kids trying to prove that they were worthy, tough, or smart. What if there is nothing to prove to anyone? What would it be like if you acknowledged and received the gift that you are within YOURSELF and didn't look for validation from anyone else or anything outside of YOU?

What if the greatest contribution to you is having an intimate relationship with yourself and not looking outside of yourself for something or someone to complete you?

With all its conclusions, this reality is really good about telling you how to be in relationship. We are fed conclusions about what a relationship is, how to be in one, how long it should last, and more! How much choice do you have if you live that way? Not very much!

What if you had total choice in your relationships and who you choose to be with? You may pretend that you have to choose what others are choosing. This is a lie. Many people believe that things just happen to them and that they have no choice. You have choice! Are you ready to be aware of that? There is choice in what you say, do, who you interact with, who you have sex with, etc.

If your relationships continue to show up the same way they always have (even when new people are involved), perhaps there is something that you love about what is showing up. What is the value of repeating patterns you don't like? I've found myself changing partners and finding the same dynamics appearing again and again. For instance, I would avoid talking to my partner when things got uncomfortable. I chose to dissociate instead of staying present, somehow thinking that by avoiding the uncomfortable situation, it might go away. Have you ever done that? Does that work for you?

To change something like this, you have to be in question about it. I would ask: Would you like to continue living this way? If not, you can ask these questions:

★ Who am I being in relationship?

★ What can I be or do different here?

What if you didn't have to recreate the same thing over and over—you had choice with creating something different? What if that something different was not how anyone else has ever created their life? What if by following what is true and real for you, you were your own leader in your life? What if a leader doesn't necessarily mean having followers? What if it created greater possibilities?

Relationships may be more than you think they are

When you think about what relationships are, what comes up for you? Are they only about relating to other people? Or is it more than that?

You can have a relationship with yourself and your body, your car or computer. What if relationship isn't what you were taught or what this reality impels on you? What if there was no separation between you, everything, and everyone else? There are lots of lies or myths about relationship. Are you willing to discover the ones that don't work for you and to be aware of them?

Your body is aware, and it communicates with you, no matter how little or how much you listen to it. When you are willing to have a relationship with your body, it can expand your life and relationships. Your body can tell you what foods to eat or not eat as well as who it would like to have sex with and who it wouldn't!

If you'd like to improve your awareness of and companionship with your body, practice talking with your body and asking it questions. Try this: When you are at the store, ask, "Body, show me which food(s) or drink(s) will contribute to you?" Then follow your awareness.

What if relationships were not significant or serious and could bring you more JOY and PLEASURE than ever before?

It may be hard not to take other people's actions and words seriously and personally, but in reality, what others do and say has nothing to do with who you are; it is simply a perspective from that person at that particular moment. It may be that someone is judging you. Could you breathe deeply and let it just be an interesting point of view, with no charge or significance? What if no one had to "get" you or your point of view? Are you willing to be that different?

Have you watched sitcoms or movies that show the countless ways people act and relate to each other? What if you were an actor or actress in the creation of your own movie? Everything and everyone who showed up in your life could be considered actors in a play and not be taken seriously. Would that perspective bring more fun to your life? As you create the script for your life, it doesn't have to reflect how you've seen others interact on television (or even how your family related to one another). You can choose who the other characters are, and how you relate to them. Would that add more joy to the creation of your relationships? Who would you like to play with?

Relationships are a Creation

Go to your local art gallery, and you will see paintings, pictures, sculptures, and/or other creative things. These tangible things you can see are creations. Some of them you may like, and some may repel you. Some paintings invite ease and relaxation. Others invite question or possibly confusion. There is not one piece of artwork that will fit everyone's life. If you saw your relationships like that, what artwork would you paint?

The relationships you have are creations, like paintings. There are blank canvases ready for you to choose and create.

269

What COLORS do you choose?

What ENERGIES would you like to embody in relationships?

Your painting may not look like any painting you've seen before. Would you be willing to paint something UNIQUE?

What if relationships were about CHOICE and POSSIBILITY rather than resentment, regret, trauma, drama, separation or judgment?

I witnessed so much resentment, regret, trauma, drama, judgment, and separation as a young boy. The adults around me didn't respect themselves and in turn didn't respect the people they were with. In their interactions, people were serious and took things personally. Watching these examples made relationships sour. I wondered why people would choose that! I've realized that was probably all they knew was possible. They did the best they could. I am grateful for my early experiences AND to now know there is always a greater possibility available.

Often people use judgment to assess who is the "right" or "wrong" person to have as one of their relationships. When judgment is present, people create separation when they've decided the people in their lives are not the "right person" they can be in relationship with. What if relationships were not created based on judgment and separation? Even if you decide there is a right person is for you, you are also judging them too. The right person you've decided you have to be with is a positive judgment. So if there were no judgment, there would be no right or wrong person to have a relationship with, just, "What will this create?"

There are choices beyond what you see and hear in this reality.

There are greater possibilities awaiting you.

Your five senses don't have to create your life—you always have another possibility.

Would you be willing to create beyond it?

What lights you up inside so much that EMBRACING it would bring you so much contribution, joy, and pleasure?

What if you created relationships as though you had no past?

At a very young age, I witnessed conclusions upon conclusions about how people should be, what they should do, and who they should be when engaging with others. How much does a conclusion limit us from being something different? What if all it takes to create something different is to start with knowing and acknowledging that you always have free will and choice, and then choose to change what doesn't work for you?

Have you noticed that many people are looking to other people to fulfill their needs? Their basic assumption is, *I need someone else to complete me.* When I was functioning from that, I felt worse when a friend or girlfriend wasn't there for me. I functioned from lack and the sense that I wasn't enough. That isn't very fun.

The relationships I knew as a young boy were about holding on to memories. People defined themselves by the memories they created; essentially, they created

272 No Matter What You Have Been Through, Anything Is Possible!

Reid Garcia, CF MW

their future from the past. Then the same thing shows up time and time again. This reality doesn't empower you to question how things have been done. It tells you to have an answer as quickly as possible, to use history as a guide, and that older people know more than kids. What if you were not defined by the past and you created something new every day? What if there was nothing to lose if we created with no past? What if memories were not significant? Are you willing to ask a question that empowers you to create the relationships and life you truly desire?

I have been grateful to have discovered the tools of Access Consciousness®, which have invited me to question anything in my life. Rather than having to function from a limited point of view and very limited choice, I now know there is a different reality available. You can choose to move beyond those points of view and create your life and relationships without conclusions.

As I have chosen to be more conscious in and with relationships, I realize there are many more possibilities than I saw as a boy. What you see as normal, average, and real is not the sum total of what is possible! Just because you haven't seen something different, doesn't mean that it isn't possible and that you can't create it. What if you created something that no one else has chosen yet? What if you know more about creating the relationships you desire than anyone else does?

From a very young age on through my teens, I made a lot of assumptions. First, I assumed that everything I witnessed others creating was all there was: struggle, hardship, pain, lack, suffering...

I thought there was no choice.

I made this reality and everyone else the guru.

What if there is no guru to look to other than yourself?

A lot of people function from no-choice and the idea that someone else is the guru. If you truly desire something different, you have to keep going, never quit, and keep demanding of yourself to know what is true for you and what you would like to create—no matter what anyone else's perspective is about it.

What if caring for you is the greatest contribution to you, everyone and the planet?

I thought that caring for others was the most important thing to do in my life. I grew up with people who had the point of view that if you cared for others, they would care for you. That is a conclusion that doesn't go very far. If you care for someone else and leave yourself out of the equation, how much caring is that for you? Very little!

If you are kind to others and don't include kindness for you, what you may create is a body that hurts and is deteriorating, a financial reality that doesn't give you all that you desire, a pattern of constantly putting others before you, regretting your relationships and stress.

Have you seen people care for others way more than they cared for themselves to the point where their health, life and money deteriorated? These folks gave and gave and gave. It was very kind of them to care for others, yet it wasn't a kindness to themselves. They focused on caring for others without including kindness for their own body or life. I have caught myself doing that at times when people would start talking to me, and I would engage and listen, even if I'd rather not. If I didn't give them attention, I thought I would be judged as being uncaring. What would it take for you to care for you? What is it like to care for you?

Let me be clear here. What I am saying about being kind to you is not about excluding anyone from kindness. It doesn't mean that you can't be kind to others.

Here is a situation that may help you look at kindness a different way. Let's say that you are walking down a dark street and a man is walking behind you. The man behind you aggressively asks you for your purse or wallet. Then you turn around and scream so loud that it scares the man to such a degree that it stops him from stealing from you and ten other people that he could have robbed that night. What if that scream is a kindness to you and to the other people who didn't get robbed?

When I neglected kindness toward myself, relationships felt like obligations. I was obligated to listen. I was obligated to like them. How much fun is it to function from obligation? No FUN—none at all! What if relationships could be expansive and joyful rather than an obligation?

Do you know more than you believe you know about relationships?

There is no one who knows what you desire in relationships more than you do! You may have been told otherwise. Do you have a desire for a different reality? You are the only one who is going to create that. No one else can do it for you. You have the joystick, and ONLY you can shift your life in whatever direction you desire.

Whatever you have going on in your relationships right now is your creation. Whatever you desire in your future will be your creation. Do you desire to keep creating the same things, or would you like something else? What would it be like to function from knowing what is best for you and that you have unlimited choice with your life and relationships?

What qualities do you desire to have with your relationships? Do you desire them to be fun, contributing, joyful? Or do you desire them to be about trauma and drama? It's your choice!

Is now the time to end the insanity of relationships and to begin the joy that relationships can offer?

Thank you for considering these ideas! I wonder what you will create?

Tools for creating a different relationship with yourself

1. *Listen to you.* Practice listening and being aware of what is true for you. What is true for you isn't necessarily what is true for someone else. Be aware if you are making someone else's opinion greater than yours. Would taking some space and going for a walk or hanging out in nature be helpful to you?

2. *Be vulnerable with yourself.* If you lie to yourself about something, you won't be able to change it,

and it will probably be a secret from you until you're ready to be aware of it. It's hiding from what's really true. What if you could dissolve the facades, masks, and judgments that you believe you are? What if you didn't have to pretend to be someone that you aren't? Being vulnerable isn't about being weak. Give yourself access to the "real you," beyond any definitions, characteristics, or concepts that you or others believe you are. There is nothing wrong with you and definitely nothing wrong with being undefinable.

3. *Be kind to you.* When you are kind to yourself, it actually invites more kindness into your life. It also allows others to see a different possibility. If there is anything that you aren't happy with in your life and relationships, be gentle with yourself! No matter what you have created up to this point, your past doesn't have to dictate your present; you always have another choice. Put your energy on what you would like to create from here on out.

4. *Never Quit!* If you choose what most don't, at times it can seem like your life is crashing or falling apart. Perhaps the old ways of doing things are dying. Keep going! The universe is here to assist you if you ask, yet you do have to choose greater and take the steps. The universe will always contribute as you make choices that work for you!

About the Author
Reid Garcia CFMW

Reid is a traveler. He loves visiting California, New Mexico, Colorado, and Italy, and wherever else is fun! He loves the adventure of traveling to keep things interesting. As a graphic artist, photographer, and videographer, Reid contributes his artistic vision toward creating more consciousness on the planet.

He also facilitates people over the phone and Skype to empower them to know that they know. You can also receive facilitation in person in his live classes around the world.

With a naturally curious sense of wonder, Reid knows that there is something different and beyond a regular life than looking at it through the lenses of the five senses.

Reid's relationship to his body has changed greatly over the last five years, especially once he became aware that he could have a relationship with it! He used to believe that the body was a struggle and hardship. By changing his point of view, he now sees his body as a playmate and a creation that can be a source of fun, joy, and pleasure.

If you would like to get in touch with him,

visit www.ReidGarcia.com

email him at dreamsinmars@gmail.com

Or search for him on Facebook under the name "Reid Garcia."

Relationship— Who the Fuck Wants That?

By Alun Jones

When I was asked if I would like to contribute a chapter to this phenomenal book about relationships it felt fun, exciting, and expansive. Despite that, I had a few doubts pop in to say hello, including, "What the fuck do I know about relationships?" and "What if people think what I have to share is crap?" Have you ever noticed that if something is easy for you, you don't even notice that you do it well? That you may know something that others don't? What would your life be like if you would recognize your areas of brilliance, and give yourself credit for them? Acknowledging your strengths and capacities allows them to expand and grow.

My take on relationships is simple: in a nutshell, know what you desire, be willing to ask for it in totality, and receive everything your choice creates. Sounds pretty straightforward, right? Yet how many people really allow themselves to know what they desire in their relationships?

Let me backtrack a bit and give you a little background.

I began life in a traditional nuclear family—mum and dad, with two children: a boy and a girl. My extended family was eight aunts, three uncles, and heaps of cousins, all ruled and presided over by my mother's mother, commonly known as "Nan." Large family, but normal, right? Doesn't everyone have such a huge family? That was what I used to think.

When I was about three years old, my parents separated and divorced. Since a couple of my aunts had also been divorced, it seemed perfectly natural to me that people don't stay together. Living with just one parent was not out of the ordinary.

Except in the 1970's, it wasn't ordinary. "Marriage is for life" was the common point of view. People disapproved of my parents for separating, and they weren't shy about showing it. Neither were they reserved about showing sympathy for my sister and me, saying, "Poor them," and "It must be awful for them." This wasn't all bad; I received all sorts of gifts and charity to help me feel better about not having a proper family. In one way that was wonderful— who wouldn't want gifts, just because? In other ways, I could totally sense their superiority and the assumption that we were somehow flawed and couldn't create anything greater ourselves. Hmmm, that felt great.... Not! At the time, I felt less than others and for years never felt "good enough." What the hell IS good enough anyway?

The situation affected me in lots of ways, not least my willingness to acknowledge just how awesome I truly am. I spent years trying to prove to myself (although fooling myself into believing I was trying to prove to others) that I wasn't useless and that I was worth knowing. I also spent a lot of time trying to push people away from me in case they found out that I wasn't as good as I was pretending to be. The insanity of it all!

When it came to relationships, other messages I grew up with were that marriage is all about give and take. You have to *compromise* and *make sacrifices*, don't you? You have to *take the rough with the smooth*, and so on. These and other such ideas coloured my way of looking at the world. Relationships involve a lot of *hard work* and *never* having everything you desire in your life because *no one can have it all.* What would make someone sign up for that?!!

Add to this the fact that many of the relationships I saw going on around me were based upon fear, unkindness, judgment, blame, shame, and guilt. Love was a tool to get people to do what you wanted them to do; it could be withdrawn any time you didn't deliver. Love was conditional. Relationships were about manipulation to get other people to do what you wanted them to do and making them wrong if they didn't. For example, my mother once said to me, "If you really respected me, you'd do what I tell you to do rather than arguing all the time." Ouch! It's the old "If you loved me you would…" And if you didn't do what the other person asked it meant you didn't love them or respect them. Another example of this was a guy who I was going out with who used to come over every Wednesday and expect to have sex. Even though I explained to him that

I didn't always want sex at 9 p.m. every Wednesday, I was told that I was selfish and uncompromising. I don't know about you, but my libido doesn't work like clockwork!

Another thing I found mystifying and slightly amusing throughout my life is the constant search many seem to be on to find "the one." You know what I mean? The "soulmate." The one who you can share everything with. The perfect match. The right person for you. Naturally, that would mean someone of the opposite sex. Remember, this was the 70s and 80s.

Boy was I confused. So I have to find a woman that I fall in love with and share the rest of my life with, making babies, and bringing them up in the virtually the same way I had been: a judgment-based reality where you can have glimpses of happiness, but you can't have it all. I forgot to say, the reason I was so confused was that it wasn't girls I was attracted to. It was boys. Men, really. I remember being totally drawn to the men my mother dated before she remarried. You can imagine that this caused all sorts of complications. My mother was a jealous and envious person and couldn't bear anyone having anything that she was unwilling to have herself. She also believed that affection and intimacy were limited, so anyone showing it to others meant she was missing out.

To add to the confusion, I had made my mother a role model. Don't get me wrong—this is not about judgment of my mother or anyone else. We were all functioning from what we knew at the time. Nobody was wrong or bad, just making different choices.

Fast forward a few years when I was willing to accept that my attraction to men wasn't a flaw or something to change. I was then playing in the playground of gay relationships. Stereotypically this means everyone sleeps around, everyone is bitter and bitchy, and relationships are something that last for a year maximum before they turn nasty and unpleasant. And then you end up very alone.

So there you have it, society gave me the message I should marry, have children, and work at the relationship through thick and thin. My mother showed me that relationships were based upon judgment, competition, blame, and shame, and gay culture typically told me I should sleep around, be a bitch to get what I want, and dump my partner after a year.

Damn! Relationships seem to be so much like sliding naked down a rocky mountain path—thrilling, exciting, and bloody painful! What a picture to paint!

I spent the first 40 years of my life looking around for the definitive "how to" guide to relationships, only to find that one doesn't exist! Everyone has a different point of view. Who'd have known? Yes, still I clung to the fantasy that there must be some step-by-step guide to having a lasting and fun relationship, and that, until I found it, I probably shouldn't stay with anyone for long.

Despite all the confusing messages and lack of a guidebook, I've been living with the same guy for the last 21 years. How the fuck did that happen?!!

One of the things I've always enjoyed and appreciated about my relationship with my partner is that we never entered into playing with each other with expectations about how long we would continue. It just kind of happened. We met, had fun, and continued choosing that.

What's changed?

Lots.

Has it all been fun? Goodness no! Sometimes it's been pure hell. For him and for me. Is it all sparkles and rainbows? No. Are there moments of stress, drama, and anxiety? Yup. However, it is a whole lot more ease and joy than ever before. Will I keep choosing it? Who knows? I am today. I may choose something different tomorrow. And so might he. Without strings attached, or fear for the future, we can live fully, moment by moment, without cutting off bits and pieces of ourselves, becoming less authentic, little by little, so the other will stay with us forever.

What I've come to be aware of in terms of having an awesome relationship with ANYONE, is my willingness to ask for everything I desire—all of the time. This doesn't mean I have to make anyone the source of what I desire. I'm just willing to ask for it. In my relationships and with every area of my life.

How many relationships are based upon compromise and trying to "keep the peace?" What if instead, they could be based upon total allowance of everything? That means total non-judgment of me and what I would like to choose, and allowance of what the other person desires and is choosing. There are times when what we desire is not the same. Does it work for us to choose something else to do together? Sometimes. Does it work for us to choose something else to do separately? Yes indeed. What is important is our willingness to ask a question. "What else is possible here that we've not considered?"

Sometimes those discussions about what else is possible can be a bit heated and so intense I just want him to shut the fuck up and agree with me! Oops! When I notice that I'm being defensive and digging my heels in further, whilst resisting and reacting with voracity (in other words being a bit of a drama queen), I ask a simple question, "What contribution can I gift and receive here?" I repeat the question in my head until I notice the situation becoming lighter and easier. It always lightens at some point. Sometimes it takes asking one or two times...sometimes a hundred! But it always does bring lightness and ease of space because asking the question creates the awareness of a different possibility or possibilities that are available.

Asking questions has been (and continues to be) an enormous contribution to my relationships and, indeed, my whole life. While asking a question invites the curiosity of a different possibility, trying to create anything from conclusion and expectations leads to a lot of stress and unhappiness. And boy did I try to make people wrong for not meeting the expectations I had of them!

The expectations we have about other people are ours alone. They are the high-speed motorway to a life of unhappiness and disappointment. Why the hell should other people live up to our expectations?! What right have we to decide what they do and how they should do it? Do you see the insanity in that? It works the other way too. I don't feel obligated to live up to other people's expectations of me, and I'm happy to be clear about that up front. What a freedom that brings!

Alun Jones

Oops, did I say that out loud? About being clear up front, I mean. For me, being totally vulnerable, with walls and barriers down, and up-front and honest about what I desire is key to creating fun and enjoyable relationships. There's no feeding them bits and pieces, so I don't scare them away by telling them too much. I desire that clarity from the person I'm in relationship with too. If they are not willing to be clear and honest about what they desire, it's just not going to work for me or the other person.

I desire a relationship in which things are always changing and expanding and one where we choose what is fun. For every area of my life, I'm choosing fun. If it's not fun, I'm not going to choose it unless there's a way to make it fun. If it's not fun, ask a question, don't just conclude. Here are some questions that open things up for me: What else can I add to my life that would be more fun? What else can I choose that will make this more fun for me and whomever I'm creating with? What else is possible here that we've not considered? What can we change about this that would make it more fun? What are we actually trying to create here and is there another way that's more fun to do that? What if we don't make ourselves wrong for not desiring the same thing?

I'd like to share one final thing about what works for me: knowing I always have a choice, and knowing that choice is limitless.

This was not always the case. For much of my life, I had bought into the belief that choice was either limited or non-existent. I could choose the chocolate or the vanilla, but not the 32 flavours. I realize now that every time I stated, "I don't have a choice," I was lying to myself. We always have a choice. We may be choosing unconsciously, or may not like any of the choices very much, but there is always another choice available. I used to have endless excuses and reasons about why I couldn't choose something. These were justifications of the lie I was telling myself that I had no choice. If I feel like I'm back in a corner with no choice, I use that as a signal to ask a question, such as, "What choices do I have available here that I've not acknowledged?" Although I don't always receive the awareness of what else is possible right away, it always comes at some point. It is always greater than the conclusions I'd previously decided we're the only possibility.

You've got to be willing to choose what works for you, 100% of the time. If you don't, you'll just resent other people. The resentment is a coverup for your unwillingness to choose what you truly desire. When you experience it, allow it to be a gift. The gift is that it's showing you where you've abandoned you in some way. You've got to be willing to receive everything and be in total allowance of everything your choice creates. That can feel like a very tall order at times, especially if the outcome is not what you expected or desired. The great thing is, you get to make another choice.

Sorry, I lied...There is just one more thing that is paramount to me and everything I choose in my life, and that is kindness. If I were to say I had a mission for my life, it is to create a world where kindness prevails, and judgment is obsolete. Kindness for ourselves as well as kindness for everyone and everything else—especially those we are in relationship with. Throughout my life, I have noticed just how unkind people can be to themselves and each other in relationships. Is it really a kindness to continually compromise and never ask for what you truly desire? Is it a kindness to the other person (people) to try and make them compromise or make them wrong for asking for and yearning for something different? Sometimes the kindness can even be to walk away. An example of this was another guy I was seeing when I was in my late teens. At the time, I was desiring a totally monogamous relationship, and that's not what he was choosing. He used to wrack himself with guilt every time he had sex with someone else because he knew that was not what worked for me. Rather than tear each other apart with blame and shame, we parted as friends with total allowance of what the other was choosing. It was the greatest kindness for us both.

When there is kindness, there is absolutely no judgment, no barriers, no resisting and reacting, no defending. There is a total willingness to choose to Be and ask for everything you desire and be in allowance of whatever your partner is choosing. That doesn't mean you have to be a doormat. That's not a kindness to you or the other person. As a coach and facilitator, I help people process things and let go of their stress and anxiety. At one point, my partner was going through a particularly stressful time at work and expected me to facilitate him every night when he got home. While I was aware he required support, it didn't work for me to be that support every night of the week, especially if I'd had a day of clients doing the same thing. We asked some questions and played with possibilities. Then we chose to talk about his work for three evenings a week, with the ability to change that at any time if something came up that required support more immediately.

A question I particularly love when there's friction or misunderstanding is, "What kindness can I be here for me and for the other person?" I wonder what the world would be like if everyone would choose greater kindness for themselves and those they are interacting with?

So there it is. A brief snapshot into how I'm creating my relationships with more ease, joy, and fun. I have no doubt if I were to write this chapter even a year from now it would be different. Everything in my life is changing from moment to moment. I am continually in the question, asking "What else I can choose that will expand my life and my relationships? What would be fun for me, and contribute to the world?"

What do you truly desire in your relationships? What would change for you if you would be willing to ask for and choose it 100%, and 100% of the time? Would you be willing to go beyond the points of view and assumptions about relationship that you grew up with so that you can create your life in a way that works for you? I hope that what I've shared here has been an invitation to that and more.

About the Author
Alun Jones

Alun Jones is a Certified Coach and Facilitator of Awesomeness! He has been coaching and facilitating since 1992 drawing upon a wonderfully diverse range of tools, questions, and techniques to empower people to embrace their awesomeness. He has one-to-one sessions with clients from all around the world, helping them to create the life they desire. He is also an Access Consciousness® Bars Facilitator where he both facilitates Bars classes and offers bars sessions.

Alun has two top priorities for his life: to create a world where kindness prevails and judgment is obsolete, and to have fun in the process. Simple. Straightforward. And totally world-changing. Alun invites you to imagine a world where everyone is kind to themselves and each other, where judgment is irrelevant and obsolete. Everything he chooses and creates is geared towards creating and actualizing that while having a huge amount of fun in the process!

Back in 2012, Alun was dealing with severe depression and was on the brink of suicide. He had already planned the day and method for how he was going to check out of his life for good. What changed that for him was Access Bars®, a modality that continues to be a total game/life-changer. One of the reasons he feels so passionate about kindness is that he had never learned to be kind to himself. For him, kindness is central to changing the world and creating sustainable life on the planet.

Alun lives in Blackheath (London, England), near the spacious Greenwich Park, where he loves to walk and spend time. He and his partner of 21 years live together in a house that they bought almost two decades ago. (They originally planned on living there for only about five years.) Interesting how things are never the way we expect them to be!

Together with Tamara Younker, Alun co-hosts a weekly radio show on Inspired Choices Network. Their show, The Playground Of Possibilities provides a space to chat, explore, and get curious about what more is possible when it comes to creating and having a life of fun.

One of the joys of life for Alun is chatting and meeting people over a good mug of coffee and a delicious piece of cake. He is one of those people that you can hear when he is around, because of his loud laugh that he will gladly express...often!

If Alun could ask you one question, he would ask you this: What kindness can you be for you and the world today that you've never been willing to be before?

Alun can be found at http://alun-jones.com

Closing Words

EXPANDING THE POSSIBILITIES

In this book, you've read about the authors' journeys, including the tools and approaches they have used to create generative, joyful relationships. Some of the chapters may have surprised you, while others may have felt like a good friend giving their advice. Now we'll focus on the most important journey: yours. Reading a book can create some change, but applying the information in your life will create much more!

Ask yourself:

What kind of relationship would I like to create?

Of the tools offered in this book, which ones appealed to me most?

_____

_____

_____

_____

What questions can you ask on a daily basis that will bring more ease and joy in relationships?

_____

_____

_____

_____

What tools or questions would you like to start using this week?

_____

_____

_____

_____

Which tools or questions would you like to explore sometime in the future?

_____

_____

_____

_____

If you have a partner, is there a chapter you would like to read with them? Would that expand your possibilities?

The next time you read through the book, it will be different! That's because as you and your relationships change, you'll see things that you may not have noticed, or that weren't as relevant to your life previously. As you write, direct, and star in your own relationship play, you create something no one else on the planet has ever created in the very same way. You bless the world by being You. Thank you for being that gift!

We would love to hear from you! How did this book touch you? What did you like? What would you like to learn more about? Please let us know so we can make improvements for future printings and offerings! Let us know about you, your obstacles, and challenges.... in fact, because you made it this far, you are a change agent! I would like to offer you a complimentary no-obligation 30 minute session to see what other changes we can rock out! My gift to you via Skype, phone, or (if geography allows) in person.

Contact me at RelationshipsDoneEasy@gmail.com or better yet, leave a text at 808-268-8708 with your name and time zone to schedule your complimentary consultation.

May your relationship with YOU deepen every day, and may you have a sense of ease and communion in your relationships, beyond anything you've ever known before.

With Aloha,

Kathy Williams